Raising

How to Raise Balanced
and Responsible Sons in
our Cluttered World
through Positive
Parenting

Contents

Introduction

This book contains proven steps and strategies on how to raise young boys with the aim of making sure they become mature, responsible, and confident as well as happy and successful in their chosen pursuits.

Raising children properly is the one thing at which any sensible parent wants to become successful. However, unlike pretty much everything else today, kids don't come with instruction manuals. In fact, no one knows how to raise children by the book because such a book does not—neither will it possibly ever—exist.

With that said, does it then mean that the parents of boys are free to raise their young charges as they please? Of course, the answer is no. Although no specific guidelines have been written, parents nonetheless need to stay within certain boundaries if they want to raise their boys properly.

This book does not claim to contain all the information that parents of boys will ever need. Rather, its main goal is to simply steer parents in the right direction as far as raising their sons is concerned. There is no one-size-fits-all solution when it comes to raising a son (or even a daughter, for that matter) because people all have different personalities. Hence, this book was written in the hope of serving as a basic guide for parents of boys regardless of what makes their sons unique.

The information herein is offered for informational purposes solely, and is universal as so. The presentation of the information is without contract or any type of guarantee assurance.

The trademarks that are used are without any consent, and the publication of the trademark is without permission or backing by the trademark owner. All trademarks and brands within this book are for clarifying purposes only and are the owned by the owners themselves, not affiliated with this document.

Chapter 1. Why Raising Boys Properly Is Important

Perhaps the most important duty any parent must undertake is raising children (After all, no one can be considered a parent unless they have even just one child in the first place.) While it may seem at first glance that raising children involves nothing more than providing them food, clothing, and shelter, and teaching them right from wrong, those are only *some* of the things parents are expected to do.

Although there have been rare real-life instances of young children who survived into adulthood literally on their own because they had no one else who will raise them, you shouldn't count on your boy being as physically, mentally, and emotionally capable of doing so (nor should you count on the world we live in being as merciful towards your offspring as it is towards those fortunate few). Not every child can grow up into a responsible adult purely through self-study. Just like in the animal kingdom, the younger members of the species will always depend on their elders to nurture them until they are old enough to fend for themselves.

In other words, children will always need adults who will raise them simply because they are incapable of raising themselves and making sure they are equipped with everything they will need to live through to adulthood. If you yourself were nurtured by your parents and other loving adults when you were younger, then surely you know better than to deprive your own children of the right to be raised in the same way.

The most important player on the team

Remember that the most important person in the process of raising your son is *you*. Only you will know what's best for him, especially since he is still at that stage in his life wherein he barely knows *anything*, let alone himself.

Furthermore, for as long as you are still around, you cannot count on a substitute to take on the responsibility of raising your son in such a way that he becomes a man of ideals and morals, and someone who is ready, willing, and able to take on the world. Besides, if you truly love your son, why would you let anyone else experience the joy and all the other emotions that come with nurturing him into someone you can be proud of?

The challenge of raising boys

As adults, we cannot deny that the boys of today are markedly different from the boys of two decades ago, or even the last decade. Boys are exposed to a lot more things today compared to the boys of earlier generations due in large part to the evolution of technology. Whereas young boys of times past grew up experiencing very little beyond the communities in which they lived, today's boys are more aware of the world around them, and the extent of their awareness would surprise—perhaps even shock—the adults of yesteryears. It therefore goes without saying that the awareness that these boys possess can be both boon and bane.

1. The proliferation of entertainment in the form of electronic gadgets that have become alternatives to studying and

playtime, video games that feature violence, and television programming with graphic images and both vulgar and suggestive dialogue have only served to turn young boys into desensitized individuals who have very little real understanding of the environment in which they live. Because they turn to these things instead of their parents and other trusted adults for guidance, they grow up not truly knowing how to deal with situations they will likely face. The consequences of lack of guidance of parents can be frightening, and many of those consequences are already being felt today.

2. The collective academic performance of boys has also suffered over the years. There is a noticeable growing incidence of learning disabilities such as reading

comprehension problems among boys. Although many of these conditions can be addressed and even corrected early on, the increased likelihood of them happening should serve as a warning for today's parents to keep an even closer watch on their sons than before.

Also within the scope of education, fewer and fewer male students finish college every year. Over the last few years, in every batch of college graduates that enter the American workforce, males have constituted no more than 45 percent. For master's degree holders, the percentage of male graduates each year is even lower. Although a college diploma is not the sole means of guaranteeing that a person will become a happy and successful working professional, the desire to pursue higher education may nonetheless be taken as a sign of a person's wish to expand their knowledge tremendously. It is thus alarming that fewer males who have taken this path successfully complete it, and the number gets smaller with each passing year.

3. Knowledge of proper interaction with others, especially adults, continues to wane partly because of the examples that today's boys see on many television programs. For example, witty comebacks have taken the place of basic common courtesy, and this has become more frequent even in cultures that have traditionally placed tremendous value on familial heritage and respect for elders. If your boy lacks the ability to be circumspect and instead habitually interacts with others the wrong way, he

may grow up not knowing how to establish and maintain relationships.

4. Even worse, there is an increase in the number of cases of physical, mental, and emotional health issues among young boys. There are various reasons for these which make it hard to just focus on a few. Otherwise, you could end up watching out for the signs of a specific issue only to find out when it's too late that your boy has been facing an entirely different problem all along.

It is indeed challenging to determine whether or not your boy is experiencing mental and emotional health issues, partly because he is still too young to adequately describe his current condition. However, with anxiety, depression, and even suicide among pre-teenaged children having become realities as well, you cannot simply stop exerting effort towards finding the proper cure or even just getting access to adequate treatment. For your boy's sake, you should never wait until something happens before you act because the unthinkable may already be happening without you knowing it.

Those are just *some* of the realities that young boys face in this day and age. With this current trend, the world of the future could become an even more challenging environment in which to raise your boy. However, just as sensible parents since time immemorial did not allow external threats to deter them from raising their children properly, you should have the fortitude to overcome whatever obstacles come your way as you equip your boy with everything he needs to be able to face the world with greater confidence.

Clearly, something needs to be done to address the aforementioned problems before it's too late. Unfortunately, though, your boy is virtually powerless to stay along the right path unless he has continued guidance from adults who are genuinely concerned for his well-being.

This is where you as a parent come in. You are here not just to love and provide for your boy, but also to make sure he grows up with the proper understanding of the world around him.

Chapter 2. What You Need to Know about Raising Boys

Persistence, patience, and unconditional love are the keys in raising children, especially boys. However, it's not enough to simply remind yourself of these prerequisites as you go about making sure your boy gets what he needs in order to have a happy and healthy childhood.

If you've been a parent for a few years now, you already know of the following truths about raising boys. Still, it wouldn't hurt to go through a brief refresher by reading this chapter, especially if you feel that you need to fill in some gaps so as to sustain whatever progress you've made. You may think of this chapter (and, come to think of it, even the entire book itself) as a sort of cheat sheet, the only difference being you're allowed to take a peek into it as often as you like. Besides, when it comes to raising your boy, you're not expected to know *everything* by heart, especially if you're still new to the experience.

You will find yourself keeping up (or trying to keep up) with him

In terms of activity, boys are almost always a handful compared to girls. Especially in the case of toddlers, boys could be sitting on the floor in the living room playing with their rattle one minute and then be climbing the desk in your study the next minute.

If you've become used to a more relaxed atmosphere at home, you have no choice but to give that up the moment your boy comes into the picture. You need to constantly be wherever he is to watch over him and make sure he doesn't end up hurting himself and damaging any part of the house. Watching over him will become less frequent when he's older, but you should never let your guard down even then.

Keeping up with your boy also means satisfying his need for a playmate at home. You should thus brace yourself for playtime that could last for hours. Also, since your boy will almost always still have a lot of energy by the time you're already waving that figurative white flag, you need to find ways to effectively manage your own energy levels and still make playtime fun and worthwhile for both of you.

You may also need to engage in sports more often than you used to do before. If your boy happens to have begun getting interested in sports even by simply mimicking the athletes he sees on television, you will be the first person he turns to for the necessary gear (i.e. balls, bats, gloves, shoes, etc.) and—more importantly—a playmate (again).

Even if you feel you are not athletic enough for some of your boy's more physically demanding interests, chances are you will still do your best to keep up with him just to make him happy. You'll be surprised at what you can accomplish when your love for him and your desire to make him happy are what motivate you.

You will find yourself answering (or doing your best to answer) A LOT of questions

Boys are curious by nature. They want to know the reason behind many of the things they see, hear, or read about. Since you are the only person who is nearby virtually all the time, you will be the first one your boy turns to when he starts looking for answers.

You don't need to make stuff up just to sound impressive to your boy. Otherwise, he will grow up with an inadequate or incorrect understanding of many of the things that go on around him, which could hurt his prospects of gaining even more knowledge and even of making new friends. Be honest enough to admit when you don't know how fish can breathe underwater or why Darth Vader wears black. Make it up to him by helping him look for the answers (and with the World Wide Web now accessible anytime from just about anywhere, you have no excuse not to be able to find what you're looking for). You can turn research into a bonding activity for the two of you, and by your example, you can encourage him to do the same when he needs to know the answers and you're not around.

Of course, if he expresses his curiosity about something you're not yet comfortable discussing with him, you can simply tell him you'll let him know more when he's old enough to understand and then quickly steer the discussion to something else that will interest him.

(Here's some good news for parents. You are most likely still a long way off from having to explain romantic relationships to your boy since he does not yet know much about the idea of expressing true love for someone other than members of their family. That gives you one less problem to worry about—for now. Still, it wouldn't hurt you to teach him a little about such relationships if only to satisfy his curiosity. Just remember, when explaining relationships, you don't need to go into detail, but you shouldn't lie to him, either.)

Sticking to just one approach won't be effective

Raising children, not just boys, is a trial and error process. More often than not, you will find that a particular approach will work wonders one day and then become much less effective the next, but it's not necessarily because you failed to exert enough effort the second time around. It's simply because you will have difficulty correctly anticipating what your boy will do next. Children are not predictable, especially when they are still much younger.

If you feel you've taken a course of action that turned out to be less effective than you'd hoped, don't beat yourself up over it. Even if you've been a parent for years, you are not immune to making bad decisions (though hopefully, the bad decisions you make do not end up hurting your son physically and emotionally). You should instead focus on moving forward and making your next steps count.

Rest assured that, throughout history, no one has yet perfected the act of raising children. All parents have had varying degrees of success, and it is not likely that anyone had ever gotten it right the first time. So don't feel that you are the only one with this kind of problem. Devote your time and energy to doing the right thing for your boy as often as you can instead of worrying for hours about how you could have fared better than you actually did.

It's a "24/7, no weekends off" job

Raising your boy does not stop just when you *think* you've done a good job; it will continue for as long as he leans on you for love and guidance (even if he doesn't overtly express it). In other words, you should spend every waking moment by making sure your son has everything he needs.

As you probably imagine, this will entail tremendous sacrifice. Other than leaving the house for work, errands, and personal commitments (like going to church), much of your time will be spent at home caring for your boy and teaching him what he needs to know. It's time to bid *adieu* to such things as after-hours sessions at the local bar with your coworkers and even regular date nights with your spouse. You can always go back to doing what you used to do for fun much later, but your boy will be a child for just a few short years. It's best that you spend those few short years watching him grow, for once those years are lost, nothing you do can ever bring them back.

There's a need to keep it simple for him (and for you)

Don't assume your boy will easily understand every single idea that you are trying to teach him, hence the need to often explain things to him. On the other hand, while raising a son is no simple task, you don't need to complicate things. You are in the process of educating a young person with barely any knowledge of the world he lives in, so you should refrain from using terms and techniques that only someone with the same education and experience as you do could comprehend.

But being simple can already work wonders. Sometimes, a hug from you is all he needs for him to feel that everything will be all right.

Your boy won't always say "Thank you"

Your boy may have a tendency to talk a lot, but there will be times when he won't be as eager to express himself. After you have taught him to say, "Thank you" to convey his gratitude, he won't always say it even if the circumstances will truly warrant it.

You shouldn't despair if it seems to you that your boy isn't as vocal about his gratitude as you want him to be. Any sensible parent will tell you that seeing continued improvements in your boy's behavior is just as satisfying as hearing him say "Thank you, mommy/daddy."

Those already serve as indicators that you have been taking the right steps in raising him.

To your boy, the most valuable treasure is *your time*

It's not the toy cars or actions figures your boy loves to play with that really mean the world to him, even though it seems he would rather spend hours playing with them than do anything else. The prospect of going to Disneyland or being visited by Santa Claus could get him all excited, but as with the toys, it's not what he really needs while growing up.

He may not overtly state it, but your boy values the comfort and security that he feels whenever you are there. He knows that you have always been there to feed him, clothe him, and chase after him to make sure he doesn't hurt himself.

However, even if you are not doing any of those things, your boy will still want you around for as long as possible.

Any sensible parent would never regret missing out on a huge raise, a coveted promotion, or a supposedly life-changing career move. They would, however, regret missing out on watching their children grow up. You will always come across opportunities that are sure to benefit your professional life, but not even all the money in the world can make up for the precious time you could have spent being with your children just when they needed you the most. Of course, you still need to earn money to provide for your family, so you cannot simply disregard your responsibility to your job, business, or whatever it is you do that pays the bills. It's just that you still need to somehow set aside a reasonable amount of time to be with the reason you have that source of income in the first place.

It's not what you've accomplished in life that matters the most to your young boy—it's *you*. Don't let your professional life take precedence over your personal life. Your family is and always will be more important to you than anything else. Let your children feel that they truly are the ones whom you love more than anyone or anything else, and the best way for you to go about this is to literally be there for them.

One simple rule: if your little boy says he needs you, *drop everything and be there for him.* If your five-year-old wants to play cops and robbers with you, pick up that Nerf blaster and let the games begin. If your seven-year-old begs for you to play catch with him in your backyard or shoot some hoops with him in your driveway, get off the couch and race him to the door, ball in hand. If your twelve-year-old asks you if you could take him fishing, that report you need to submit to your boss on Monday can wait even for just a few hours.

You wouldn't want to end up spending your later years regretting not being there for your boy, worrying about precious moments that you know will never happen again. You can somehow make up for lost time, but it will never compare to spending as much time as you can with him while he still needs you more than ever. For your boy, the time is always *now*.

You won't always be there no matter how badly you want to

The reality is that your boy will eventually have to learn to stand up on his own just as you yourself have once done. Therefore, you cannot always be physically present to show him the way in his later years. It is inevitable that he will make judgment calls by himself and live with the consequences of his decisions whether good or bad.

How then do you ensure that he will be equipped with everything he needs to face the future? You help him prepare for it in the present. While you are still able, you need to devote much of your time and energy to instill greater confidence in him by guiding him in everything he does.

The only drawback with this is you wouldn't really know whether or not you were successful in preparing him until his later years when he will have become fully aware of the gravity of many of the decisions he makes. Still, you cannot simply say you've done all you could for him and then just hope for the best. You stand a much better chance of helping him gain greater confidence in standing up on his own by continuing to guide him as often as you can before he becomes old enough to finally leave the nest.

Chapter 3. Proper Conduct at Home

Your home is the environment where your boy
will spend much of his time aside from school.
As such, it is but logical to make the best use of
the time that both of you are safe at home to
instruct him on how to act appropriately in any
situation.

Because young boys get easily distracted, it is
best to teach your boy about proper conduct at
home wherein the environment—as well as
virtually everything that goes on in that
environment—is within your control. You can
easily move potential distractions out of the
way temporarily so that your boy could devote
his attention to you and whatever you will teach
him.

Teach him basic proper manners

As soon as your boy is able to talk, he must start to learn saying things like "Please," "Thank you," and "I'm sorry" depending on the situation. If these and other polite words and phrases are among the first words he uses regularly, it will become easier for him to adopt the habit of being courteous towards others even as he grows older.

You can get him to practice saying those words as often as necessary through his daily interactions with you and everyone else at home. For example, if he forgets to say "Please" when he asks you for a glass of milk, gently remind of what he needs to say before handing him his milk. It is mainly through constant expression of these short but well-meaning phrases that he picks up the habit of saying the right things at the right times early on.

Manners also include rudimentary etiquette like the proper way of eating and keeping one's voice down, especially while indoors. It will be quite challenging at first to get your boy to properly comply with these and other basic rules regarding correct behavior. However, if you persist in showing him what he should do and in correcting every deviation, he will ultimately get the message and learn to put what he has learned into practice without being prodded to do so.

Also under this is proper deference towards others, especially elders. As a child, your boy may have gotten used to the fact that he easily becomes the center of everyone's attention, especially when you have guests over. Your boy will likely do anything just to continue getting everyone present to notice him. It may seem adorable at first, but if you do not keep a close watch on him, he could end up being disrespectful yet be completely unaware that his words and actions are beginning to aggravate others.

Everyone else will not overtly say it since disciplining your boy is your responsibility and not theirs, but you shouldn't wait until someone finally comes up to you and says your little one needs to tone it down. Take the time to remind your boy of the importance of giving other people a chance to be noticed for a change. Teach him to learn to give way once in a while since he will always have his own opportunities to get people to notice him anyway.

Enforce the household rules strictly but fairly

Your boy is the most important thing to you, and so you will likely be willing to forgive and forget every time he does something contrary to whatever household rules you have established. However, you need to be firm and show your son that your authority as a parent is beyond debate by strictly enforcing the rules. That means for every time your boy does not follow the rules, he will receive a corresponding punishment, like not being allowed to watch TV after he has done his homework or having his toys kept well out of his reach for an entire day or so.

It is imperative that you implement the proper penalties every time you are aware of an "infraction" committed by your boy. Otherwise, he will gradually realize that you are not really serious about denying him certain privileges when the situation warrants it. If that happens repeatedly, it will become harder for you to discipline him since he knows he can sometimes get away with his disobedience.

Make household chores fun

Your boy would unsurprisingly have a natural aversion towards anything he doesn't perceive as enjoyable, especially if he would end up tired from doing it (Playtime is not the same thing as he would still want to keep playing or running around the house even when his body begins showing signs that he needs to rest.). Doing the chores is no exception. Even older people would rather do something else, yet they admit doing the chores will almost always take precedence because of the benefits.

One way of making the idea of doing the chores more appealing to your boy is by adding a little fun to the otherwise boring activity. You could turn certain chores into "minigames" such as shooting balled up socks in the laundry basket as if you were shooting hoops or putting his toys back in the toy chest like a mission in a video game that he needs to complete within a set time. A search through the World Wide Web will give you countless ideas on how to make your boy more enthusiastic about helping you around the house.

You could entice him further by rewarding him with a bowl of ice cream, dinner with him at his favorite pizza restaurant, or longer playtime upon completion of a set of chores for one day. You don't have to spend too much on a reward, though. Any reward will do for as long as it helps instill in your boy a sense of accomplishment at having completed his assigned tasks for the day. Later on, you can get your boy involved in doing the chores without necessarily giving him anything material in return. Over time, you should be able to get him to see how he himself could directly benefit from doing things like washing his plate and utensils when he's done eating and making sure his toys aren't strewn all over the living room floor.

Doing the chores helps instill a proper work ethic in your boy. By getting him to do some of the chores at home, you are teaching him that not all things come without cost. It is the first step in teaching him that if he wants to have a comfortable life, he will have to work for it.

Of course, the chores you will let your boy handle should be appropriate for his physical build. For example, it wouldn't be a good idea to let your son take out the garbage if he is not yet big enough to wheel the refuse bin out to the curb without unintentionally tipping it over along the way. Also, you should never ask your son to do something that you aren't willing to do yourself. For each chore you want him to be able to perform on his own, you need to show him how it's done, do it together with him, and then gradually let him take over as you keep a constant eye on him and intervene as needed until he gets it right.

It will be a learning experience for your boy and an eye-opener for you. You want him to be able to stand on his own in his later years, but you will realize that part of you still would want to keep a close eye on him even then.

Become a role model to him in every way

With your boy seeing you around the house pretty much all the time, it becomes inevitable for him to adopt some of your mannerisms. You must therefore make sure that whenever he sees you, you are doing something that you would have no problem seeing him do himself.

Just as in teaching him to do the chores, you should lead by example. You can spend the whole day explaining to your young boy how he needs to behave in certain situations and why, but unless he sees it in practical application, he will not fully understand the ideas you want him to learn. The same rule applies to your language. For example, if you don't want your boy spewing profanities every time he gets frustrated, then you'd best not do the same, even when he's not around. You can still explain to him that there are people who are not as mindful as they should be about their words and actions. Just don't forget to tell him that it's not okay for him to be just like those people because what they're doing is wrong.

Don't wait for the right person to show him how it's done because the right person for the job is *you*.

Limit his exposure to media

In this day and age, television programs can and do serve as a form of entertainment for young boys. At the very least, watching television can help keep them too preoccupied to run around the house just when they need to be quiet, such as when you're taking a much-needed afternoon nap. Cartoons and other child-oriented television programs can even help keep boys entertained and may even be sources of important life lessons for them.

However, watching television should not be treated as the only way for your boy to keep himself entertained. There are plenty of other ways available to him, and some of those have been proven to be more effective in teaching children valuable lessons. As a parent, you are responsible for making these alternative means readily accessible so that he will learn not to regard television as the outlet he should immediately turn to whenever he gets bored.

Also bear in mind that not all television programs that seem to be child-friendly on the surface actually feature child-friendly themes, scenes, and language. In fact, many of today's most popular animated television series are more oriented towards mature audiences. They are technically cartoons, but they feature adult situations to which young children should not be exposed. It therefore pays to do enough research about the programming available in your region before allowing your boy to sit in front of the television.

Also, it is not wise to allow children who are still at this stage to be active on social media, so don't even think about allowing your boy access to social networking and video sharing sites. Although the more reputable of such sites claim to enforce strict censor rules to ensure their content is relevant, informative, and wholesome all at the same time, a number of shrewd subscribers still somehow get away with promoting content that could warp children's perception of the world around them and, in turn, their way of thinking.

Your son is still getting the hang of properly interacting with others face-to-face at this stage. Don't make the mistake of allowing him to explore the online world while he is still coming to grips with interacting with the people who are always around him such as his family, his teacher, his friends, and his classmates.

Chapter 4. Proper Conduct in Other Settings

Of course, it is inevitable—and actually necessary—for your boy to go out of the house regularly, especially when he reaches the age at which you plan to start having him go to school. It is at this stage that he will begin interacting with people other than his family almost every day. It goes without saying that he needs to be prepared to properly handle these situations as well.

Despite your best efforts, though, you cannot totally shield your son from situations that could potentially have a negative influence on his thoughts and actions, as well as situations wherein he has no one to rely on but himself. As mentioned in one of the earlier chapters, no matter how much you want to, you will not always be there to tell him how he should act. However, you can already begin laying the foundation for proper conduct before he goes out into the world that lies beyond the four walls of your home.

Teach him to be empathetic

Many of the bad things happening today stem from people being too selfish to be sympathetic to the plight of others. Hence, if your boy sees another person who may seem unpleasant at first, you would want him to try to think of every possibility, including the possibility that the person concerned appears the way they do through no desire or fault of their own.

If you and your boy come across something that he doesn't normally witness at home, like an elderly woman in tattered clothes, sitting on the sidewalk, and begging for spare change or scraps of food, explain to him the possible circumstances behind what he has seen. Tell him something like "Maybe she has trouble finding a job," or "She might have a family but they probably couldn't take care of her anymore," instead of "She's out here in the streets begging because she's too lazy to work for a living."

Furthermore, you don't need to make it seem as if your assessments are the correct ones. You are simply teaching your boy not to quickly judge other people prematurely based purely on what he sees. You are also teaching him that other people could end up in certain circumstances without anyone else ever really knowing why, and so he must learn to have an open mind when dealing with them.

Encourage him to see the good in things

Bringing your boy out into the world exposes him to different things both good and bad. The bad things he sees may seem to outnumber the good ones, but with your help, you can train his eye to be more observant and perhaps gain a better understanding beyond what a first glance can ever reveal.

While he's still young, you should already have him started on this by getting him to pick up the habit of seeing the good in everything. Of course, you need to constantly guide him every time you go out so as to give him a glimpse of as many different situations as possible, and then try practicing on each one. For example, if it's raining heavily where you are, making it nearly impossible for people to stay outdoors, you can point out the fact that at least the plants are getting enough water. If the two of you end up stuck in a traffic jam that prevents you from getting to your planned destination without delay, you could use the time you are stuck on the road as bonding time instead of getting angry because of the inconvenience it caused you.

By teaching your boy to look for the bright side to everything, you take the first step to instilling in him the important human trait of positivity, which will serve him well as he grows up. If he makes a habit out of focusing on the positive, he will become more proficient in dealing with, and overcoming, difficult situations. He will have very little time to be frustrated or angry because his mind is focused on identifying every possible benefit from a seemingly negative event.

Show him the importance of body image

Being well-dressed and properly groomed is an indication of people who take good care of themselves. As such, your boy should always look his best whether he's going to school, seeing his pediatrician, or accompanying you at the supermarket. We all know, though, that appearance takes precedence over comfort in this case, so don't be surprised if your boy starts to fidget and express his annoyance about being made to wear that new collared shirt that you picked out for him because he feels he would much rather be in his Spider-Man costume.

Firmly but gently tell him that he needs to dress according to the situation, especially when he gets older. Tell him he can still look "cool" even if he doesn't look anything like his favorite superhero. If he needs proof, show him that everyone else does it, including his family and friends.

One way of making him more enthusiastic about this is giving him an opportunity to decide for himself. Before you go out for the day, you can go through his closet, take out only those clothes you would want him to wear, and let him choose. You may need to do this regularly to get him used to the fact that there are ideal clothes for every situation. You could also take him with you the next time you go shopping for clothes for school, church, or Saturday afternoon at the park and help him pick from the available selection.

At this stage, your boy is not yet old enough to establish *his* own fashion sense and that is why he depends on you to guide him in this aspect. If you constantly help him choose the clothes he wears, the concept of dressing appropriately for any situation will gradually but firmly take root in him, and will remain with him even as he gets older.

Teach him how to greet and acknowledge other people

It goes without saying that many of the basic manners you taught your boy at home will be put to good use here as well. Specifically, your boy should be taught the importance of showing respect to other people by greeting them with a sincere smile and acknowledging them, especially if they have helped him in any way. Even someone who seems to be in a bad mood may be greeted in this manner. Who knows, maybe that small gesture of kindness can help them even temporarily forget about what's making them feel miserable.

It's not hard to imagine what the world would be like if everyone was polite and courteous towards each other, and your boy needs to picture that as well. Show him how it's done by doing it yourself as you greet people you come across every day. You may need to gently remind him of what to do in case he forgets to greet someone properly, but with enough persistence on your part, he will surely pick up the habit.

Teach him to offer help to those in need

Part of the learning process of interacting with others is showing others that you can be relied upon in case they need your help. Your boy therefore should learn this as well, and there's a huge chance he will carry this sense of obligation with him through to adulthood after having learned and practiced it habitually during his younger years.

Doing good deeds for others without expecting anything in return is a common trait of those who have been regarded as some of the most influential people in history—Dr. Martin Luther King Jr., Saint Teresa of Calcutta, and Mahatma Gandhi just to name a few. Their wish to make the world a better place for their fellow human beings far outweighed any desire they may have had for wealth, and that is why they remain highly regarded even many years after their passing. Hence, if your boy wants to be truly remembered, he should make a name for himself not by amassing riches, but by offering assistance to those who need it.

Of course, you shouldn't just tell your boy to offer help to other people unless you are willing to do so yourself as well. If you are able to adequately explain it to him through your actions, he will get a clearer idea of what is expected of him whenever he faces such situations. For example, if you and your boy see an elderly man struggling to bring his groceries to his car, approach him and offer to assist him. He may decline the offer, but if he states that he does indeed need help, you and your boy shouldn't hesitate to take some of his shopping bags and accompany him to his car.

If the kind old gentleman is generous enough, he may reward your boy—like, say, in the form of a candy bar—to show his appreciation (You may need to teach your boy to politely decline any rewards from time to time so that he won't come to expect it whenever he lends a helping hand.). Otherwise, if all that come from him are a huge smile and a "Thank you" or even if he doesn't thank you at all, you should remind your boy not to be upset about it and instead be contented at having made another person's life a bit easier even for a few minutes.

If a person asks your boy for assistance, your little one should at the very least acknowledge that other person and then either exert the necessary effort, or politely decline and say that he is presently unavailable to help. On the other hand, if your boy sees a person who clearly needs help despite that other person not having said it overtly, your boy should be the one to initiate the encounter by asking if the other person needs help. In other words, your boy should learn to be proactive as well.

Remember to teach your boy that he should only assist in instances wherein his physical ability will allow him to easily lend a hand. For instance, much as he really wants to, he simply cannot provide much help for a neighbor who's trying to move something as heavy as a refrigerator up a flight of stairs.

He should know what it really means to be a winner

It is at this stage that your boy begins participating in team sports whether in your community or as part of gym class in school. You may have probably realized by now that even casual games of basketball and soccer can become highly competitive as different boys who want to become known for their athletic prowess keep on doing their best to make sure their respective teams come out as the winners. Taunting the other team is a possibility, and so is getting physical. However, just because they're still kids, it doesn't mean they can get away with these. If left unchecked, these can surely open the door to unsportsmanlike conduct being more frequent as they get older.

You should teach your boy that there is more to life than achieving first place. While it is indeed important for him to strive for greater accomplishments by making the best possible use of his talents, you should stress to your boy the importance of being kind, even if he has bested others in competition. He should learn to focus less on winning and more on giving his best, working properly with his team, and making sure he doesn't intentionally hurt anyone whether physically or verbally.

Childhood is that stage in your boy's life wherein he should still have fun and not yet worry about winning, so don't let his quest for the trophy rob him of the genuine joy he can derive from the mere act of participating in his favorite sports along with his friends.

He should learn to embrace failure, too

The idea of "winning at all costs" has been unnecessarily accepted as normal in many social circles. Although it can serve as an effective motivator under certain situations, it puts tremendous pressure on young children (especially boys) who are yet to discover where their true potential lies. Because winning has become the only goal for the team, losing is regarded as a sign that one is not good enough. Thus, there are such occurrences as blaming one particular individual for causing their whole team to lose the game.

Teach your boy early on that this kind of thinking is wrong. No one deserves to be humiliated for losing because every game may have only one winner. Perhaps everyone had worked their hearts out and yet it was the other team who won anyway, which isn't exactly uncommon. The best thing anyone can do in such a situation is to charge it to experience and strive to do better next time.

Even if your boy's team fails, he should learn not to beat himself up over not attaining something for which he prepared and worked so hard, even if someone else says otherwise. Give him a feeling of hope from knowing that if he failed in one instance, he might win the next round, or the next one, or the one after that. He'll never know unless he persists.

The same applies in activities other than sports, like in a school spelling bee or in a local talent contest. He should graciously accept failure for it helps strengthen his confidence to take on greater challenges as he gets older.

Chapter 5. Assisting in Your Boy's Academic Development

It was discussed in the first chapter of this book that boys have been gradually falling behind girls in terms of academic performance every year. Learning disabilities can in fact be overcome, and addressing these disabilities at their onset—or even before they start to manifest—gives parents a better chance of helping their boys become successful in school.

Even if you are not an educator by profession, you still have a role to play in ensuring your boy's educational growth. The good news is you are, by default, a player in a small but close-knit team that also consists of your boy and his teachers, and your goal is ensuring your boy is better able to retain whatever he has learned, not just help him get good grades. You can fulfill your role in this by following the tips discussed in this chapter.

Talk to his teacher

The only person who can speak with certainty about how your boy is performing in school is his teacher. Your boy's teacher will give you a rundown of the areas wherein your boy is doing well, but you can expect that they will also share with you the areas where your boy is not performing up to par. Before implementing any of the succeeding tips, it is important that you first get detailed feedback from your boy's teacher.

You should also maintain open lines of communication with the teacher, especially if your boy needs help with his studies. With his teacher regularly updating you on his performance, you will be better able to gauge whether or not your chosen approach in helping him learn more easily is effective.

Encourage him to love reading

Many of the common learning disabilities among boys are related to reading comprehension skills (or rather, lack thereof). However, many experts believe constant practice will have a significant positive impact that will prevent these same disabilities from gaining a foothold. By constant practice, it of course refers to habitual reading of lengthy content of useful information. In other words, your boy needs to make a habit out of reading and of being able to understand what he has read.

You can get started on helping your boy foster a love for reading even before he starts going to school. As an alternative to his daily playtime, the two of you can pick out a short book that you could read to him. The book may even have images that can grab his attention if words can't do so yet. Even the act of reading your boy a bedtime story before he goes to sleep every night is a step in the right direction. Don't wait for him to ask you to read to him every night. You should always be the one to initiate the action.

Your boy doesn't need to know how to read just yet to be able to appreciate the process. In the beginning at least, you could regard reading time simply as bonding time for the two of you, as well as a way of helping him turn it into a habit he can practice even on his own. By the time he is old enough to read basic words, you can continue guiding him by helping him look up the correct pronunciations and definitions of words that are unfamiliar to him. This is, of course, another habit he needs to be able to practice on his own, and your constant guidance in the beginning will gradually motivate him to learn to do it unassisted.

It is also believed that no one who owns a library at home ever got bored. If you don't have a big enough collection of books at home, your next best option is to bring him with you to your local library regularly. Help him find books that might interest him and read along with him. Instead of getting him toys as birthday presents or as rewards for doing the chores or attaining good grades in school, you may want to consider getting books and magazines for him to read. Whether it's at home or at the library, if your boy has plenty of books readily available to him, he will have plenty of ways to use his free time more productively than by watching television or playing video games.

Also, some of the books your boy reads do not need to be educational in nature for as long as their content is child-friendly and he enjoys reading them again and again. Even when he enters adulthood, he will engage in reading purely for leisure as a way not only of gaining new knowledge but also as a means of "practicing and perfecting the craft."

Guide him as he does his homework

When your boy starts going to school and he starts getting homework almost every day, don't expect that he already knows the answers or even where he should look for them. Although it is not explicitly stated, parents can help their children with the homework while at the same time remind them that they will have to learn to eventually do it by themselves.

If he's working on some math problems, don't give him the answers right away in case you already know those. Guide him through the process of solving for the answers in order for him to practice his skills. If he's having difficulty finishing a reading comprehension assignment that also includes questions that determine whether or not he understood what he has read, help him look for the relevant portions in the text. You may even need to rephrase the given questions to help him more easily provide the correct answers. Whatever it is he needs to do, you should be there to show him the way.

It goes without saying that you can treat homework as another bonding activity as well. Your boy will always remember your willingness to spend time with him and help him accomplish something that he doesn't find enjoyable. Your presence can serve as a sort of safety net, reassuring him that it won't be impossible for him to look for the answers because you will be immediately available to come to the rescue.

It is not expected that you will always be available to help him with his homework (especially years later when he will be living far from home, like when he finally starts going to college). Your goal here is to instill confidence in him so that he will know how to look for the answers on his own. Still, you should strive to devote as much time as you can to helping him with his studies while he is still young enough to easily adopt the habits that will serve him well.

Invest in games and toys that will stimulate his brain

One other way of making your boy more enthusiastic about learning is introducing him to board games, toys, and other similar tools that can make the prospect of studying more attractive to him.

These are not the same as the big blocks with letters of the alphabet on all sides that many of us played with when we were kids. There is actually a wide range of recreational learning tools available on the market today, each one devoted to a specific learning skill or a particular school subject. For example, if your boy seems to be having difficulty in mathematics, you can let him play with games that help develop arithmetic and problem-solving skills.

These games and toys have always been regarded as far more practical alternatives to video games and other forms of entertainment that not only fail to teach valuable lessons that may be applied in everyday life, but also cause children to spend far less time than they should for studying, exercise, and other more worthwhile activities. For one thing, these games and toys don't run on electricity, which means they can be played anytime, anywhere. Your boy can play with them during his free time after he has done his homework and his share of the chores. He can even play them when you travel so that he won't easily get bored during long trips.

Another benefit of educational games is that they open the door to customization. Specifically, parents may opt to come up with their own versions of popular children's games, modifying these in such a way that help improve learning and studying skills while being fun and entertaining at the same time. The World Wide Web has plenty of references on DIY educational games, hence allowing you to easily look for ideas on how to make learning more appealing to your boy.

If your boy still insists on being allowed to play games on a computer or a mobile device, you can compromise by allowing him to play mainly those games that will enhance both analytical and creative thinking in children. A quick search of the World Wide Web will lead you to reputable developers of mobile apps that can help foster learning by expanding one's vocabulary, reinforcing problem-solving skills, and improving memory retention just to name a few.

Consult a specialist if necessary

If you have done all you could to help your boy in his studies and yet his performance in school continues to suffer, he may require the services of a child behavioral specialist to determine the true extent of his learning impediments. The assessment of your boy's academic aptitude will help determine if he is to continue studying in the same school and with your present home study setup, if he will require the assistance of a tutor as well, or if you need to explore the option of alternative education that is better suited to his learning ability.

It is imperative that you accept the assessment with an open mind instead of allowing your emotions to cloud your judgment. Otherwise, if you fail to adequately address the issues regarding your boy's academic performance simply because you chose to ignore the facts, you could very well end up depriving him of valuable opportunities for further educational development.

Whatever happens, you should never give up on your boy. Don't feel that he has no more hope of doing well in school simply because the conventional approach wasn't as effective as you had hoped. You should instead keep on exploring all possible options to ensure he keeps moving forward academically, even if his pace might be considerably different from those of other children his age.

Chapter 6. Dealing with Bullying

Bullying has become a common occurrence in various social settings, from schools to workplaces and everywhere in between. It has taken on a number of different forms, the most extreme of which include inflicting physical injury on people who are unable to defend themselves. Chances are you already know about individuals who have been permanently maimed or who have been driven to take their own lives just to put an end to the bullying.

There is of course nothing positive about bullying, despite the clamor to have it outlawed having come about only in recent years. In any case, childhood bullying is not some rite of passage or just another way of testing of one's potential to grow up into a "real" adult. It is plain and simple harassment and humiliation at the hands of another person, and no one would ever want to go through this experience even once. If you truly love your boy, you will exert more effort in ensuring he is safe from being picked on by others. You cannot be there for him all the time, but you should still do your part as a parent in preventing him from becoming another potential statistic.

If the bully is another child in the neighborhood, then you can simply tell your boy to avoid him. He could just ignore the bully or choose to play with another group of kids. However, if the bully studies in the same school as he does, he will find it difficult to avoid being harassed by someone he is likely to meet almost every day.

If your boy has already become a victim of constant bullying at school, or even if you simply suspect that he is slowly turning into a victim, you should take action right away by following these steps.

Get him to talk to you about it

If your boy comes home to you crying that he is being bullied at school, drop whatever you're doing and sit down with him. Let him settle down first so he can regain his composure enough to be able to speak coherently.

Otherwise, if your boy has not told you outright that he is being bullied but you nonetheless see the signs, be the first to talk. Don't ask your boy if he is being bullied. Simply ask him how he is or if there is anything wrong. You may need to prod him until he tells you everything, but until he does, refrain from doing anything else like bringing the matter to anyone else's attention.

Also, don't limit yourself to yes-or-no questions. The questions you ask need to be answered by your boy in greater detail so that you would truly know his side of the story.

It is important that you do not let your emotions cloud your judgment even though it becomes difficult for you not to be affected, especially if it breaks your heart just to listen to your boy relive his experience at the hands of someone who takes pleasure in making his every waking hour miserable.

Reassure him that it's not his fault

Show your boy that, above all, you do sympathize with him and you are just as eager as he is for all this to go away. Tell him that he has done nothing wrong to warrant this kind of treatment. Reassure him that this kind of thing happens every day even to older people, and it's just his misfortune that a bully chose him as a target.

He may want to get back at the bully (Don't deny it; some part of you wants to get back at the other boy, too.), but patiently explain to him that revenge is not the solution. Promise him that you will personally talk to his teacher about it so that they can help put a stop to the unpleasant encounters.

Remember what was discussed earlier about a warm hug being the best remedy for your little boy? There isn't a better time for you to give him one, so wrap him in your arms and tell him to let it all out. Show him that he is safe in the knowledge that you will comfort and protect him when no one else can.

Talk it over with his teacher

The first authority figure you should talk to regarding your boy and his encounters with the bully is your boy's teacher. With schools across the country having declared zero tolerance against bullying, you are sure to find a sympathetic ear the moment you bring the matter up with his teacher.

You should first assume, though, that the teacher knows nothing about the bullying incidents. Otherwise, they would have called you first to notify you that your son is being bullied. Either way, you should explain the situation to them so that they will know the effect it is having on your son's self-esteem.

There is no need for you to advise the school on what needs to be done as it is likely they already have a protocol to follow whenever situations like this occur. As part of the protocol, they will ask the bully to give his side, and you and your boy may be required to provide proof of the bullying as well as witnesses. At this point, you can't help but feel like you're participating in a police investigation instead of a disciplinary meeting at school, but unless there is proof of bullying, it is not likely that the school will initiate any action to ensure your boy is better protected.

If the bully is proven to be at fault, it is likely he will get a formal warning as well as a reprimand discouraging him from harassing your boy any further. Your teacher will also probably be instructed to keep a closer eye on both children concerned during class hours.

If all else fails, transfer your boy to another school

If your boy tells you that the bullying is still going on despite the official reprimand from the school, contact his teacher right away to inform them. In the event that the school is still unable to prevent your boy from being bullied, you may need to have him study at another school (or even homeschool him if you have the necessary credentials). Taking him out of his current school may be costly, and not just in terms of money, but there's really no point in allowing him to stay in an environment wherein the adults who have been tasked with guaranteeing his safety keep on failing to do so.

Remember, you should not continue to put your boy's well-being at risk just because it is inconvenient for you to pursue alternative options.

Encourage him to do his part as well

If your boy is not being bullied but has been a witness to bullying in his school, he should learn to take initiative by letting people in authority know about the incident if the child being bullied is too scared to do so. He needs to bring it to the attention of his teacher right away, especially if he personally saw the bullying as it took place.

Just like when he lends assistance to others, your boy should not expect any reward for following his conscience. He will learn to derive true happiness and a sense of fulfillment from having helped another unfortunate child.

Chapter 7. Caring for Your Boy's Mental and Emotional Health

As you have probably realized early on, this book will not discuss physical health as there are already plenty of references on the topic. Instead, this volume will talk about mental and emotional health, partly because a large number of parents today are still at a loss as to how they can ensure that their children grow up with sound minds and hearts.

You don't really need statistics to convince you to take your son's mental and emotional health seriously. The truth is he is just as vulnerable to mental and emotional problems as the next child, even if he seems to be in a cheerful mood every time you see him. You thus need to be willing to look beneath the surface to know what really lies there and then help in making sure your boy gets the treatment he truly needs.

Know the signs of anxiety and depression in children

Children are not immune to the effects of anxiety, though in their case, the manifestation is generally milder compared to that of adults.

Anxiety in some forms may be deemed normal in young children, like in the case of separation anxiety that your boy will experience when he first goes to school. He will of course refuse to leave your side as he believes he will not be able to feel your love and nurturing when he is not in the same place as you are. He will eventually overcome this anxiety with your help (and the time will come when he feels is old enough that he becomes embarrassed whenever he is seen with you). However, anxiety is no longer considered normal if it interferes greatly with your boy's day-to-day life. If his fear of or aversion towards something is so great that is causes him to essentially "shut down," you as a parent will easily see it.

Furthermore, it's important not to immediately dismiss mood swings in children, especially if the instances of such last for unusually long periods. Dr. Marilyn B. Benoit, MD, former President of the American Academy of Child and Adolescent Psychiatry, states that parents have every reason to be concerned if their children's apparent moodiness seems to last for more than 2 or 3 days, which is normally how long it would take for a mentally sound child to easily recover from a trivial negative experience. That, Benoit claims further, could be an onset of clinical depression, and it will potentially have a significant adverse impact on his studies, his interaction with others, and even the way he takes care of his body:

- He will be irritable and grumpy towards others, even his own family.
- He will more easily get exhausted.
- His sleeping patterns will become alarmingly inconsistent.
- He will have difficulty concentrating while he's studying and even when he's pursuing worthwhile hobbies.
- He will become less and less confident in himself.
- He will start to lose interest in the things from which he used to derive enjoyment (i.e. sports, watching television, playing with his toys, etc.).
- And—worst of all—he will begin harboring thoughts of hurting and even killing himself.

With clinical depression now also often befalling children below age 19, you should be ready for the challenge of helping your boy deal with that possibility if he is at risk of suffering the same condition.

Consult the right specialists

Before doing anything else, you should find out if there are child psychologists, psychiatrists, and other licensed experts on child and adolescent behavior in your community. It is best that you discuss with these specialists what your plans are regarding your boy since they can properly guide you every step of the way.

As with virtually everything else that concerns your boy, you should never leave anything about his mental and emotional health to chance. Do not assume that reading a ton of books on the topic will give you all the knowledge you will ever need to effectively monitor your child's condition and provide remedies before potential problems can escalate. You must instead trust these experts who have spent years studying and working on cases involving children as part of their job description.

You should work with your boy's doctor to identify what could be the reasons for his condition and to come up with a treatment plan that is most appropriate for him in light of the home and school environments in which he interacts every day. You also need to keep them updated on his progress.

Continue cooperating with these specialists even as your boy consistently shows signs of improvement. Remember, even a seemingly minor setback during treatment could have farther-reaching adverse effects if left unchecked.

Help your boy manage the symptoms

Your boy's therapist is the foremost authority on his treatment, but that doesn't mean they are the ones who will do all the work involved. Regardless of the treatment plan recommended by his therapist, you as a parent can help facilitate your boy's recovery from the debilitating condition he is suffering from by incorporating simple changes in his day-to-day routine. The good news is these methods do not involve any expensive medicines or invasive procedures. In fact, these are simple approaches wherein he receives increased quantities of some of the things he needs in order to live: sleep, healthy food, and exercise for both body and mind.

Supplemental treatment options for your boy include but are not limited to the following:

- *Getting at least 8 hours of uninterrupted sleep every night.* Studies have shown that anxiety and other mental disorders have been linked to lack of sleep. Hence, your boy needs to get enough sleep to recharge his brain, hence giving him improved concentration and memory retention over time. Remember, a refreshed mind will leave less room for anxiety and depression to gain a foothold.

- *Eating food rich in protein.* Consider changing your boy's diet to include more sources of protein, without which the brain's neurons cannot effectively "communicate" with each other (by sending enzymes, hormones, and neurotransmitters back and forth). A steady influx of the right amount of protein can have a positive effect on your boy's emotions and cognitive function, making it easier for him to dismiss those thoughts and emotions that could cause him to "shut down." Ideal sources of protein include lean meat, whole grains, fruits, vegetables, and legumes.

- *Regularly engaging in physical activity.* Getting the whole body working for at least 10 minutes will release a significant amount of endorphins, which are the body's "feel good" hormones. If your boy does this often, he stands a better chance of recovery. Just make sure that the physical routine you want your child to engage in is sustainable enough for the long term so that the two of you will enjoy doing it again and again, exhaustion notwithstanding. It can be something as simple as the two of you going for a walk around your neighborhood for 30 minutes 3 to 5 times a week.

- *Practicing mind relaxation techniques.* Encourage your boy to regularly perform meditation and other relaxation exercises even if he is not feeling stressed or anxious. Studies have shown that regular practice of meditation can be beneficial for the so-called "gray matter" in the brain that is linked to sensory perception, memory retention, emotions, decision making, and self-control among others.

It is recommended that you inform your boy's therapist of the supplemental treatment you want to implement in order to manage the symptoms of his condition. They might recommend additional activities for you and your boy to perform at home to further augment his ongoing treatment.

Conclusion

Thank you again for reading this book!

I hope this book was able to help you gain a better understanding of what young boys need from their parents as well as how to raise them into happy, healthy, and successful adults.

The next step is to apply what you've learned from reading this book and to share it with others. The information featured here can even be used by your own children in the future when they decide to start raising families of their own.

Don't limit your knowledge to what has been written in this book as it is merely a guide and not the last reference you'll ever need. As such, it is recommended that you also read other references on the topic of raising boys. There is no such thing as "too much information" when it comes to raising a child, so make the effort to gain as much knowledge as you can from trusted sources and from people who are already a long way down the road you are traveling now.

Also, the most valuable resource available to you will be your own experience as a parent. It is what you will always fall back on as you spend the remaining years of your life raising your boy into someone who will be truly happy and successful while making the world a better place in his own simple way.

Thank you and good luck!

Raising Daughters

How to Raise Balanced and Responsible Daughters in our Cluttered World through Positive Parenting

Introduction

This book contains proven steps and strategies on how you should raise your daughter so that she will eventually become independent, smart, hardworking, and—most importantly—always confident in herself and in her ability.

Have you wondered if you're making the right decisions when it comes to raising your daughter? Over the last years, there has been a lot of confusion about the role of girls and boys. It's easy to see why parents are left with lots of unanswered questions when they're raising their children.

Raising a daughter is no easy task, especially with so many outside influences that threaten to instill in girls beliefs that could prevent them from having—much less achieving—dreams that are truly worthwhile. Thus, among our responsibilities as parents are continually showing our daughters the way to true success in life and reminding them to focus on what's really important and not be obsessed with trying to conform to the world's ever-changing standards of beauty.

Lastly, to borrow the message in that popular song, our daughters are beautiful in every single way and no matter what other people say. They should therefore learn to be confident because they are already beautiful and so have no need to prove themselves for others' satisfaction.

The information herein is offered for informational purposes solely, and is universal as so. The presentation of the information is without contract or any type of guarantee assurance.

The trademarks that are used are without any consent, and the publication of the trademark is without permission or backing by the trademark owner. All trademarks and brands within this book are for clarifying purposes only and are the owned by the owners themselves, not affiliated with this document.

Chapter 1. Not Just Princesses

Our daughters are indeed the proverbial embodiment of sugar, spice, and everything nice—and more. That's why we, as parents, need to totally commit ourselves to making sure our little princesses will grow up happy, healthy, and as safe as possible from all the nasty things around us. We should also help them grow up with the inner strength they need to take on bigger challenges on their own. In other words, they should be princesses who are warriors as well (Think Wonder Woman and Xena—and to a slightly lesser extent, Leia Organa from the *Star Wars* films.).

For starters, this chapter will present to you a brief guide on what you can expect as you raise your little princess into a queen ready to take on the world.

Young girls crave for their parents' attention

There's a simple reason why you happen to always see your little girl nearby regardless of what you're doing, especially when both of you are at home—she just wants to spend time with you. The 1-10 years old bracket is typically the stage in girls' lives wherein they love even just being with their parents, especially their fathers. Your little girl will crave for your attention, and you should be ready, willing, and able to give her precisely that.

It is important that you keep acknowledging your daughter's presence, especially during that stage in her life wherein she will always want to be noticed by you, as this will help her develop her feeling of self-worth. The more often that she receives this acknowledgement from you, the more it reinforces her belief that she is indeed an important person, and therefore worthy of others' respect regardless of what she does.

As your daughter gets older, she'll likely spend more time with her peers and often keep to herself while she is at home (probably on the computer or using her phone), and you will realize by then that you will have missed out on valuable opportunities for interaction if you did not give her your time just when she needed it the most. Thus, you should not make the mistake of thinking your little girl needs you only when she is faced with a situation that is too difficult for her to handle—let alone overcome—on her own. The truth is your little girl needs you *all the time*.

You don't necessarily have to stop what you're doing to devote your full attention to her, especially if what you're doing is important (like finishing an urgent report for work or fixing a leaky kitchen faucet). You don't have to get her directly involved in it, either, especially when she is not yet capable of helping you out. It will be enough for her if you simply let her watch you closely as you go about your task and engage her in small talk every few minutes. Don't hesitate to respond, especially if she asks you a question (even one not directly related to what you're doing at that moment). The important thing is you show your little girl that she is indeed important to you by giving her enough attention regardless of what you're doing.

Girls' biggest role models are their mothers

This is not just a manifestation of the classic notion of "Girls gotta stick together." It is actually almost natural for young girls to look up to the people who are with them virtually all the time, in this case their mothers (Obviously, it's the fathers in the case of families where the mothers are the breadwinners and thus have to be at work every day while the fathers bear the brunt of managing the affairs of the household.). Even if they claim that their idols are famous celebrities or simply other girls they know in school, it is inevitable for daughters to follow their mothers' example in many of the things they do.

Daughters will observe how their mothers react to different situations. If girls see their mothers have a habit of responding negatively to unpleasant situations, like using harsh language or hurtful retaliatory actions, chances are they will regard these as the normal way of dealing with such situations. And it's not just *what* their mothers do that will be ingrained in them; it's also *how* their mothers do things. For example, if a mother has a tendency to act on impulse instead of evaluating the possible consequences before she makes a decision, it's likely her daughter will act in the same manner even when she gets older. Therefore, it's necessary for mothers to exercise utmost prudence as they think, speak, and act in order for their daughters to know the proper way of living their daily lives, especially interacting with other people.

However, mothers should not expect that their daughters will turn out exactly like them. For example, just because a mother is more of a logical thinker does not mean her daughter won't be far more creative in doing the same things. Parents should therefore learn to embrace their children's differences from them for as long as these differences won't bring any harm upon themselves or others.

Girls' fathers determine their standards of men

A father provides more than love and care for his daughter; his personality will also give his little girl an idea of which qualities a man should possess. Even if a father doesn't tell his daughter outright what she needs to look for in a man (such as when she is assessing whether or not a male acquaintance would make a good romantic partner), she will nonetheless spend a lot of time observing his speech, actions, thoughts, and mannerisms. The more frequently that a daughter sees particular traits in her father, the more likely these will be ingrained in her memory. Even if she is taught otherwise as she gets older, chances are she will still look for those traits simply because she grew up having regarded them as normal (and therefore acceptable).

The obvious danger here is that she might also regard as normal in men those traits that actually do more harm than good. A study conducted by the National Institutes of Health in 2003 established a correlation between unplanned pregnancies and a lack of a strong father-daughter relationship. A separate study done by the Texas Tech University's Department of Communication Studies in 2008 revealed weak father-daughter relationships also increased a woman's propensity to make poor decisions, enter into destructive romantic relationships, and have strained interactions with their peers. Hence, if a father wishes for his daughter to enjoy better relations in the future, most especially with people who will truly respect her (and whom she will respect in return), he needs to be a living and breathing example of the kind of partner she deserves to have in her life. Even if his daughter decides not to get married and settle down in her later years, a father is nonetheless responsible for showing her how she needs to be treated by members of the opposite sex.

(If the father is not a part of the daughter's everyday life while she's still young, then there needs to be another trusted adult male role model like an uncle, a grandfather, or a neighbor.)

You'll sometimes find yourself at odds with her

Girls are highly observant of the world around them. It's impossible for them not to form their own opinions of the things to which they are exposed every day. Even just a chance encounter with something or someone can already get them thinking about the emotions that the encounter made them feel.

This, however, can be a double-edged sword, especially when your daughter enters her teen years. Because she will feel the "many years" she has lived will have already taught her enough about dealing with life's ups and downs, she will tend to have her own idea of how some things should be done, which won't necessarily benefit her in the long run. That includes the manner in which she is being raised to become a mature, responsible adult. Hence, you should prepare yourself in case she expresses disagreement with your views on nurturing, career goals, and discipline just to name a few.

In any case, you should be persistent in guiding her through her formative years. Don't let a few differences in opinion dissuade you from being the kind of parent she needs—one who loves her, understands her, and accepts her for who she is.

Their admiration for others could start even before they enter their teen years

This could be a good thing or a bad thing, depending on how you as a parent see it. In any case, though, you need to keep a close watch on your little girl to make sure she maintains her focus on more important things like her studying, developing her confidence, and learning how to properly deal with different people and situations.

Fathers especially have every right to be concerned once they realize the full implications. There's an old saying that states that a father's worst fear is knowing his daughter could someday meet someone who is as wild and as crazy as he was when he was seventeen. Thus, any father in his right mind would want his little princess not to rush into things, but rather to wait until she has a good chance of meeting a Prince Charming who is mature enough to respect her and love her for who she is rather than for what she can provide.

Chapter 2. The Challenges of Raising Daughters

Our daughters indeed need a lot of guidance and nurturing if we want them to grow up into the women they are meant to be. However, it won't always be smooth sailing when it comes to raising them, especially in this day and age when a lot of factors could adversely affect their development into mature and responsible adults. As you go about raising your daughters, it would be to your advantage and hers that you become more aware of the three biggest issues that you will face in fulfilling your responsibility as a parent.

Today's girls tend to take greater risks

Many parents of girls today attest to the fact that their daughters seem to be bolder—or rather, bold enough to do things they themselves weren't confident enough to do before. This is due in large part to girls becoming more aware of the world around them (thanks to the proliferation of technology) compared to girls of times past. The obvious downside to this is that they may be unknowingly getting themselves into situations that could do them more harm than good simply because they initially perceived these to be worth trying out. By the time they find out they are putting themselves at risk, it may already be too late.

With that said, it pays to be available as much as possible to answer whatever questions your daughter may have about the ever-changing world and her place in it, especially when she enters adolescence. Don't hesitate to talk to her about subjects you did not feel comfortable discussing before such as sex and relationships, all the while firmly reiterating where you stand on them.

If your daughter seems to purposely avoid such discussions, you should nevertheless be persistent and find a way to drive the message home. Otherwise, if you give up after she repeatedly avoids talking to you about sensitive topics, she might end up formulating her own understanding of such issues without being fully aware of the negative consequences (which could often be serious in nature).

Remember, a parent's guidance and enlightenment can play a significant part in helping a child navigate through these challenging times and make it out in one piece.

There is an overwhelming need for them to be "cool"

Have you noticed how many young girls today seem to be obsessed with the way they look, hoping that they would get noticed? And have you also noticed that these girls often seem to keep stocking up on things like clothes, shoes, makeup, and accessories? In fact, they seem to have a greater propensity to spend on such items than do adult females who can more easily afford those (and who have a greater need for such items).

Noted psychologist and parenting advice expert Steve Biddulph places the blame for this on evolving trends in marketing and advertising. After professional advertisers arrived at the conclusion that the preteen and teenaged girl consumer markets have been largely ignored for the longest time, they decided to overcompensate. They accomplished this by promoting certain products in such a way that young girls would feel that they've been missing out on things they actually needed all along. The result is a growing number of girls becoming convinced that fitting in and getting people's attention were more important than setting goals for themselves and accomplishing them, and so they keep falling all over themselves getting in on the latest trends in the belief that it would get them the attention they think they need.

Girls are not immune to low self-esteem

Girls may be emotionally stronger than boys are, but that doesn't mean they can easily overcome issues with their self-esteem, especially feelings of emptiness and worthlessness. This feeling of inadequacy can also last through to adulthood. In fact, even some of today's most successful adult women are humble enough to admit to the rest of the world that they are still trying to overcome that feeling, with varying results.

Mental health issues seem to hound young girls as well. A study conducted by the Maryland-based Substance Abuse and Mental Health Services Administration showed that young girls are three times more likely to suffer from depressive episodes as boys are, and this greater tendency has been found to be linked to self-esteem problems that first manifest during the preteen years.

(There is a number of steps that you could take to help your daughter successfully deal with her confidence issues. The good news for you and your daughter is that the entirety of the succeeding chapter is devoted to precisely that purpose.)

Regardless of the challenges our daughters face (and regardless of the challenges we as parents face in raising them), they deserve the best possible care and nurturing during their formative years. It is therefore imperative that we totally commit ourselves to this endeavor to make sure our little girls grow up strong-willed, confident in themselves, and eager to provide help to those who need it.

Chapter 3. Giving Your Daughter that Much-Needed Confidence Boost

We discussed in the previous chapter that a growing number of females have reportedly suffered from a feeling of inadequacy that often begins to manifest as early as childhood and can last through to adulthood. This negative feeling can remain strong in a woman even after she has received all manner of accolades that attest to her proficiency in any field, whether it's business, sports, politics, or entertainment and media. This only goes to show that it takes more than physical awards or similar indicators to make a woman genuinely feel that she is indeed a valued and esteemed member of society. In fact, any woman deserves to feel valued regardless of what she has achieved.

It is up to you to get your little girl started on the road to discovering her true worth. When the two of you succeed in this, she will have the confidence she needs to overcome challenges, including the tougher ones she will face when she gets older. It will also give her something she can always fall back on during those times when others fail to even recognize her for the good that she does.

Make her feel that she matters just as much as everyone else

Making your daughter feel more confident about herself starts with showing her through your words and actions that you appreciate even the simple fact that she is there. One way you can easily practice this is to simply acknowledge her every time she comes up to you whether you're busy cooking dinner, reading the paper, or working on your car. Satisfy her curiosity by showing her what it is you're doing and explaining to her why you do it. Through it all, remember to use a gentle tone and a few terms of endearment as you welcome and accommodate her. Even a simple "There's my little sugar plum!" or "What does my little sweetheart want?" will suffice.

Being affectionate through your words can already work wonders for your little girl during her formative years. By your interactions with her, she learns that she deserves respect from other people even if she doesn't do anything for them, and so she will grow up in the knowledge that she is worthy of respect regardless of how popular she is among her peers. When she is aware of this, she knows that she should not have to go to great lengths just to get people to respect her and that she should not expect others to do the same for her just to be worthy of her respect. In other words, she will realize that she matters and that other people matter too regardless of who they are.

You don't have to go all out just to make your daughter feel that you truly appreciate her being there with you. You simply need to make her feel that she is indeed a part of your everyday life by getting her involved in the things you do. It could be something as mundane, like, say, scrubbing the bathroom floor. You could make her participate in the activity by showing her how to do it and then perform the chore together.

You obviously can scrub the floor without asking for help from anyone, and your little girl will only be shouldering an almost negligible portion of the labor anyway. However, by getting her involved, you are showing her that you value her participation even though you know she physically can't do much towards accomplishing the task at hand. Making her feel that she is needed can do wonders for her confidence (It could even help instill in her the courage she needs to face rejection, especially in her later years.), so you have to do this as often as possible while she is still young.

Compliment her often

To any little girl, her parents are her number one fans. With that said, you will expectedly be the first person your daughter turns to when she is in need of praise, so don't skimp on it.

Complimenting your daughter should not only entail praising her appearance; it should also involve all the other things that make her special. Your daughter needs to learn early on that it's not just her looks that people will be talking about (This will be discussed in detail in a later chapter.). Teach her to understand that she can also be recognized for her intelligence, her creativity, her skills, and her passions. She must learn how to develop these as well so that she will know how to deal with different situations wherein her appearance—or even her being a woman—will have no bearing at all on the eventual outcomes.

Praise your daughter as necessary, but remember to focus only on the real things that actually deserve compliments, like getting a C on a rather difficult math test or the fact that she helped your elderly neighbor carry her groceries to her porch (or, when she's still little, that she was able to go potty by herself). Use short, simple words she can easily understand so that she will still not easily forget your praise even long after the fact. This will give her a feeling of fulfillment as well as motivate her to keep doing the right thing in any endeavor she undertakes.

Remember not to go overboard with praising her or else you could end up voicing your approval for things that don't really warrant it. For example, you won't accomplish anything by telling your little girl "That's a lovely dress you're wearing today!" as a spur-of-the-moment way of cheering her up after she gets eliminated from the school spelling bee. What you should instead do is compliment her for having done her best and then remind her that there will always be other opportunities for her to showcase her talents to everyone else.

Even as she gets older, you should keep complimenting your daughter whenever necessary. You will always be her number one fan, and so she will continue to value your opinion even if she starts to seek validation from people outside of family as well.

Put her emotions first

In letting your daughter know that she truly matters to you, it is important that you are not in a grumpy mood whenever she interacts with you whether she is cheerful, sad, or even irritable. Even if you've just had a horrible experience at work or on your way home, you should never make your little girl see your ugly side, especially when she is not yet at that stage wherein she possesses a better understanding of people's different moods.

Be sensitive enough to put your daughter's needs first. Do your best to maintain a jovial mood as you interact with her at home. Otherwise, if you snap at her while she's in a jovial mood herself, you could end up giving her the impression that her feelings are not that important and that she is not allowed to express herself freely.

If you really believe that you need to deal with your emotions first by letting them out or doing something productive until the negative feeling subsides, you can simply tell her "Sweetheart, Daddy/Mommy needs a few minutes alone. I'll be with you later. Is that okay?" Your gentle tone and your reassurance that you will make time for her afterwards will compel her to leave you alone temporarily to deal with your thoughts.

Once you're ready, take the time to listen to her talk about her day, and if something has made her upset, give her a warm hug and tell her it's okay to let it all out. Reassure her that she can freely talk to you about what's on her mind whether it makes her happy, sad, or angry.

It would be foolish (insensitive, even) to tell your daughter to simply brush off any negative feelings whenever she experiences something that has made her sad or upset. She should be allowed to express how she truly feels instead of being told not to be bothered by it and to just move on to other things. Otherwise, it will only reinforce the negative notion that her feelings aren't important enough to be heard. If she grows up thinking that keeping her unpleasant emotions all bottled up inside is the normal thing to do, then she will have difficulty in forgetting hurtful experiences and in focusing on making the most out of each day she has been blessed with.

You should also cherish the moments while your daughter still sees you as her only sounding board because when she gets older, she is likely to also start sharing her thoughts with people other than you (although recent studies show that older girls are still more likely to talk to their parents—especially their mothers—before talking to anyone else about their problems, emotions, etc.). It is thus important that you give your little girl enough time and opportunities each day to speak her mind.

As your daughter gets older, you should little by little make her realize that she should also learn to give others a chance to express their emotions just as you let her express hers. It won't always be about her, and so she needs to know when to give way and let others have their turn. You should also reiterate that not everyone she comes across will be as accommodating as you are when it comes to letting her express herself. Still, she should not let this cause her to simply remain silent and keep her emotions bottled up inside. There will always be a time and place for her to freely express herself, and with enough guidance from you, she will *always* know when the right time and place will be.

Teach her how to handle rejection

Adorable as your little girl may be, the fact remains that she will not always be welcomed by people she wants to get to know better. Not everyone will see in her the same precious little angel that you see, and so she needs to understand early on how to effectively deal with rejection.

Rejection actually starts to occur as early as childhood. Some of the more common examples are not being picked to play as part of a sports team and not being invited to a party at a close friend's house. Young girls who experience these and other instances of rejection would tend to feel unwanted and unsure of their worth, especially if they are not reminded that they are still important to a select few people (i.e. their parents).

Teach your daughter that rejection happens all the time, even to grownups. Grownups might see themselves as more knowledgeable and more capable in certain areas, and yet they face harsh realities such as not being accepted into their preferred schools, being repeatedly passed over for promotion at work, and having someone they love leave them to be with other people. By sharing with her these examples, you make her realize that being rejected doesn't mean she is not good enough. It's just that some things aren't meant for her no matter how much she feels she deserves them.

Whenever your little girl experiences childhood rejection, be quick to tell her that there is something better in store for her, but no one knows yet what it is or when it will come. She just needs to remain hopeful until then and not let the instances of rejection dampen her spirits. She also still has to express how she feels, after which she can move on to doing worthwhile activities that can reorient her focus and help her better overcome any negative feelings instead of dwelling on the unpleasant memory for longer than necessary.

Remember, your little girl is still at that stage of life wherein she has the freedom to do whatever makes her happy virtually whenever she wants. She therefore shouldn't let the experience of a few temporary setbacks linger in her memory every day.

Embrace and encourage her uniqueness

In the years leading up to adolescence, your daughter will spend a lot of time trying to find out the person whom she wants to be. This happens almost naturally instead of being the result of her deciding on her own that this is what she should be doing. One of the reasons is her exposure to other people and situations, and this exposure also encompasses the times she is with her parents (especially her mother). If she starts to notice how people are different from one another, she will form the impression that she should have her own identity as well, and it is up to you to guide her into becoming the person she is meant to be.

Any parent will of course have their own expectations of their children, but those expectations should not be too overwhelming to the point that they deprive youngsters of the opportunity to explore what is available to them. Although you still need to teach your daughter right from wrong as well as the basics of proper manners including how to act in public, you cannot impose upon her your ideal vision of whom she should be, even if you believe that it is for her own good. Rather, you should observe which direction she is taking and find out how you can help her develop her chosen identity while teaching her to become a person who will respect others and who is worthy of others' respect.

You don't have to be as enthusiastic as your daughter is about where her interests lie in order for you to fully appreciate them. All your daughter needs is for you to understand and accept her decisions and trust that she will turn out all right.

Being able to choose her own identity will serve as your little girl's emotional foundation now and in the future. If she is more aware of her identity early on, she will not be easily convinced to try experimenting with different personas until she finds one that she hopes will pass other people's scrutiny. She doesn't have to strive to become the most popular girl in class if she already knows that she can still be happy by simply being Little Miss Bookworm. And when she enters high school, she doesn't need to endure long hours of cheerleading practice if she is far more comfortable actively participating with her friends in the photography club. Anything will do for as long as she is happy with it.

Guide your daughter into finding her own place and she will realize that she can be happy by standing out, not by fitting in. Even if she later on adopts an identity that is worlds apart from her previous one, she will at least know that she will be making that change because she wants to and she is comfortable with it, not because someone else told her to.

Don't shield her from stumbling and falling

Somewhat ironically, your little girl will learn to develop her confidence early on if she experiences failure and disappointment from time to time. Over time, allowing her to feel all the emotions associated with things not going her way will gradually help her become more resilient and able to focus on getting it right next time or accomplishing the next important item on her list. Otherwise, if she does not realize early on the gravity of failing to successfully finish an important task, she will be unable to cope with difficult situations on her own and she will end up *always* having to depend on others for support. Because this will always put her at a disadvantage after she has finally left the nest as an adult, you obviously would not want it to happen.

When your daughter suffers a setback like flunking a test in school, it's not enough to simply praise her for having tried her best. It is important for you to also make her understand why not getting a passing mark can make anyone who studies hard feel bad. After she feels the corresponding emotion and realizes what she needs to do next, she can more easily devote all her energies to working on her areas of improvement and striving to achieve more favorable results at the next opportunity. This will serve her well should she encounter even bigger disappointments such as not being accepted into her college of choice and failing to close a deal with an important client. After all, how can she learn to successfully bounce back from an unpleasant experience if she has no unpleasant experiences to bounce back from?

You would not want your daughter to feel inadequate, but you also wouldn't want to overdo it to the point that she is getting praised even in instances wherein she obviously could have done better. Thus, while she's still young, it is important that she understands all that is associated with things not going according to plan.

Chapter 4. Looks Aren't Everything

When she's still young, your daughter will start to do things like put glitter on her nails, wear bracelets, necklaces, and other fancy kids' accessories, and brush her hair a different way every few days, all with the aim of making herself look pretty. This is purely harmless fun at this stage of her life as she merely wants to see how a different look would suit her, or maybe she just likes to mimic some of the people she interacts with regularly (like her teacher or one of her older female relatives) or those she watches on TV. There is nothing wrong with letting your little princess do some experimentation with the way she looks (for as long as she doesn't hurt herself or leave a huge mess in her wake).

As your daughter grows older, though, looking pretty will gradually become a way of getting other people's attention and validation, and so her approach to that end will become more deliberate and more precise. Whether she wants to become accepted (or, at the very least, not shunned) by the other kids in school or to be noticed more often by a boy she admires, she is likely to do what is necessary just to make sure she will be nice enough to look at. It is at this point that you must start taking an even closer look at her motivations as well as her methods. Otherwise, your innocent little angel could later end up going to extreme lengths to make herself the center of everyone's attention, but in a bad way and for all the wrong reasons.

You may have probably noticed that young girls feel themselves coming under ever-increasing pressure to look beautiful—or rather, to look more like what most of the people around them *think* is beautiful. The two are obviously not the same thing, partly because people have differing definitions on what makes a person physically attractive, and so it would be impossible to become beautiful in the eyes of *everyone*. However, a number of girls continue to be overwhelmed by the need for validation, and this is mainly because of a feeling of inadequacy that has been plaguing them for years.

The noticeable corresponding changes in motivation and methods will manifest even as early as the initial stages of adolescence. Among these changes is the increasing use of methods that promote weight loss. In fact, a number of studies have revealed that a growing number of girls aged nine and ten have admitted to trying to lose weight while other studies have shown a bigger percentage of teenaged girls have been regularly resorting to riskier weight loss methods (such as laxatives, diet pills, and even starvation diets and other forms of unnecessary fasting) even though they possess perfectly healthy bodies. Dealing with childhood obesity is one thing, but losing weight just for recognition (even through harmless methods) is quite another.

The clothes that young girls are fond of wearing will also come under scrutiny at this stage. The worldwide entertainment industry is awash with female celebrities that many younger girls look up to, especially with regard to how they dress. The biggest problem here is that many of these individuals are so popular even among girls who are not yet in their teens that they end up inadvertently encouraging these youngsters to dress in public the same way they do, which isn't always within the acceptable limits of decency. The same is true with individuals whose popularity is limited to much smaller groups, like in the case of the "cool girls" in many schools throughout the country. You have every right to be concerned if your daughter happens to pattern the way she dresses after an individual in her school who is known for wearing rather revealing attire for someone of her age.

It is alarming that many young girls who are still at the stage wherein they are supposed to enjoy life with very few worries are already beginning to harbor an unhealthy obsession with making themselves look even prettier, believing it to be the only way for other people (including those whom they barely even know) to recognize and accept them. Thus, there is no reason for parents to simply wait until their daughters are old enough to fully understand the danger that comes with trying to become attractive purely for the sake of getting noticed. Our little girls need to be reminded while they're still young that there is more to being beautiful than simply *looking* beautiful.

Remind her that she is—and always will be—your beautiful princess

Before doing anything else, it is important that you make your daughter understand that not having a slim body and "movie star looks" will not necessarily make her unattractive in case she feels she does not possess those and other associated traits. Teach her that each one of us is special and unique, including those people who don't seem to get even a little attention. We all have differences that allow us to excel or at least be recognized in certain aspects. Otherwise, if all of us were the same in everything, then we wouldn't be able to enjoy the satisfaction that comes from being unique as well as use it to help us get ahead in life. As the old saying goes, "If everybody's special, then nobody is."

While she is still young, you should keep showering your little girl with affection to make her feel that there is someone who already sees her as beautiful even if she doesn't do anything to change the way she looks. You should do this most especially during those times that she is sad, like when she feels she is not as pretty as the other little girls she knows. Tell her that there isn't any part of her that needs changing, and so she shouldn't worry about whether she is good enough for other people. Remind her that she *is* good enough and that it's not her fault if others can't see the attributes that make her stand out above the rest.

Even if your daughter isn't into typical "girl stuff" such as dolls, tea parties, and stuffed unicorns and she claims she is not a princess but would rather be "one of the boys" and play video games and go catching frogs, she nonetheless deserves to feel your loving affection every single day. Whatever your little girl is interested in, she still needs to be reminded of her inherent value that places her above everyone else in your eyes.

See who her role models are

It pays to know whom your daughter sees as her inspirations when it comes to the way she looks. Does she admire a popular female actress, singer, or musician? Or does she want to fit in with some of the "cool" kids in school by adopting the same getup and hairstyle that they do? At this stage, you should enlighten her on what is okay and what is "too much" with regards to imitating the people she idolizes.

It's okay if she wants to change her regular ensemble because it could be easily done anyway. If she wants to dye her hair a different color, you could tell her that since the effects are longer-lasting, she can do that when she's older and when she's not likely to keep changing her mind and sport a new color every time. However, if your daughter's role models happen to be rather "extreme" in terms of their preferred look, like habitually wearing clothing that is a bit too revealing), you need to convince her of the merits of staying just the way she is and of why it would not be in her best interests to simply do as her idols do.

Pave the way for her

It was also mentioned in the first chapter of this book that many young girls consider their own mothers as role models. If you are a mother to a young girl, chances are your little one is taking hints from you as far as appearance is concerned. There is therefore a possibility of her mimicking the way you dress even with whatever clothes she has in her closet. Conversely, if you yourself have often felt sad or frustrated because of how you look, chances are your daughter will follow suit.

If you are a mother and you want your daughter to be proud of who she is and to do something about her appearance only when necessary, then you yourself should be willing to do the same. Lead by example by being proud of who you are and what you have. Don't let your dress size or your weight dictate the way you should feel about yourself, especially if you and your daughter are of a certain body type that you may have difficulty changing (unless you resort to drastic and possibly harmful practices, which is obviously not advisable).

Show your little girl that there are far more important things than being beautiful in others' eyes, like being kind towards others, intelligent, and hardworking. Remind her of people who achieved great things despite not having "ideal" attributes like slim figures or perfectly contoured faces. When she learns to respect herself and others regardless of how she looks, she will understand that true beauty stems from her sincere effort to make the world a better place and not from how others see her.

Encourage her to stay within acceptable limits

Of course, your daughter still needs to look her best in any setting. Thus, it wouldn't hurt for her to incorporate a few harmless improvements to spruce up her everyday appearance. She can treat this as an outlet for creativity and self-expression, which are essential in her personal development. When you give her just enough freedom to choose the clothes and accessories she will wear as well as what look she will sport, you will enable her to practice skills that can serve her well in her later years. Specifically, this exercise teaches her to pay attention to even the smallest details and to make adjustments where necessary in order for her to have a fresh new look every time without doing anything drastic.

Remind your little girl that looking her best should entail nothing more than wearing the appropriate clothes and a modest selection of accessories, as well as being properly groomed. She can still be adorable in others' eyes without being flashy or seemingly desperate for attention.

Teach her not to judge others by their looks

Just as your daughter has been taught not to exert any unnecessary effort in trying to look prettier in others' eyes, she also needs to be taught not to form her opinion of others based simply on their appearance.

For example, if your daughter tells you that she and her friends always avoid this one girl in her class because she wears old and dirty clothes every day and she looks like she doesn't brush her hair at all, gently remind her that that girl she is talking about might not be at fault for how everyone else sees her. You can tell your little one that maybe that other girl's parents can't afford to buy her nice clothes or that their home environment probably makes it difficult for her to devote enough time to properly grooming herself. You could even encourage your daughter to get to know this other girl a little better even if she is at first reluctant to do so; chances are she just might make a new friend she can happily spend time with both in and out of school.

And it's not just those people whom your little girl at first sees as unattractive that deserve closer scrutiny (as well as greater understanding). You also need to show her that even those who seem to pass every known standard of beauty can still possess dispositions and behaviors that will make them less desirable to be around. Your daughter should not get the impression that the only good people in this world are the "beautiful" people, but on the other hand, she shouldn't completely avoid certain individuals even after she finds out they aren't as friendly as she initially thought. Teach her to be willing to be kind to everyone, even those who aren't likely to reciprocate the gesture.

At the end of the day, your daughter needs to realize that a person's appearance isn't the only way of determining their worth and that everyone deserves to be scrutinized fairly beyond how others see them.

Bonus tip: It pays to stay fit

Although girls don't really have to go to great lengths to look attractive, there is still a need for them to be physically healthy. For example, it's understandable if your daughter does not want to lose weight since she's already confident with who she is and therefore feels no need to change her stature to please others. However, just like everyone else, she still needs to live a healthy lifestyle that incorporates a proper diet, regular exercise, and enough hours of sleep every day.

It's not just physical health benefits that can be gleaned by staying fit. Your daughter can also enjoy mental health benefits such as lower stress levels, reduced risk of anxiety, and improved concentration. With conditions like obesity and depression now more common even among children who are not yet in their teens, it is never too early for your daughter to get into the habit of taking proper care of her body without necessarily being able to make people turn their heads.

Remember, being beautiful both inside and out is possible only for those who know how to take care of themselves first.

Chapter 5. Make Education a Priority

Studies conducted in recent years have shown a disturbing trend; there is a growing gap between adolescent girls and boys when it comes to academic performance with girls in general leaving boys well behind. There have been more instances of boys suffering from learning disabilities from as far back as their early elementary years. Furthermore, among those who finish college in the United States, the ratio of boys to girls gets smaller every year, and even fewer males go on to earn graduate degrees.

Does this mean then that you have nothing to worry about because you are confident your little girl already has an edge (over boys at least) with regard to education? Of course, the answer is no. It would be ridiculous to expect young girls to effortlessly become geniuses or even "just" consistent achievers on their own. From kindergarten to high school (and even beyond), they still have to be guided into taking the necessary steps towards attaining the education they need to succeed in their chosen fields. As a parent, you should thus always be ready to provide your full support in making sure your daughter devotes the necessary time and effort in securing a proper education and, in turn, a bright future.

Encourage your daughter to have her own dreams that she will attain someday

While your daughter is still young, it is important for her to have an idea of what she wants to be when she grows up. Even if it remains to be seen whether or not she will indeed achieve what she originally aimed for, having a concrete goal early on can help her maintain focus as well as motivate her to study hard and make proper use of her knowledge and skills. Otherwise, without setting any goals for herself, she is not likely to become as serious about studying as you would want.

Of course, her dreams need to be realistic as well. For example, it's still cute and amusing to listen to your three-year-old girl proudly tell you and other people that she wants to someday go on adventures with her friends under the sea (likely a result of her having seen one too many Spongebob episodes), but it's no longer amusing if she's still singing the same tune when she's older and her science classes in school have already enlightened her on why pretty much everything that happens in cartoons is impossible in real life.

Set high educational expectations for her

Setting high educational expectations here means having the confidence that your daughter will successfully attain all the educational prerequisites for her chosen career. This goes beyond helping her in her studies and in developing the skills she will need to achieve passing marks on her own. It also entails having faith in your little girl's ability even without telling her outright.

It could also easily work the other way, though. A Wake Forest University study revealed that having negative expectations about your children is likely to result in your worst fears as a parent coming true. For example, if you keep thinking that your daughter won't finish high school, there's a huge chance that that is precisely what will happen even if you intervene to help her achieve the more favorable outcome. Hence, in your every waking moment, it is important that you are confident that she will become what both of you want her to be—a happy and successful adult working professional.

Help her set the groundwork for her chosen future career path

After your daughter has decided on what she wants to become in the future, you should then help her orient her focus towards a specific educational track that will significantly increase her likelihood of attaining her dream job (This should ideally begin no later than her high school years, which is the point where she needs to decide whether to continue with her education or enter the workforce, specifically in jobs not requiring a college education.). In other words, you should guide her in choosing educational courses that will endow her with the skills and knowledge she will need to qualify for—and ultimately excel in—the job she wants to have someday.

It must be stressed that helping your daughter prepare for a particular career path early on does not mean she will have to stick with her original plan no matter what happens. For example, just because she proclaimed when she was younger that she wanted to become a celebrated doctor, you cannot expect that she wouldn't change her mind a few years down the road and decide to instead become, say, a hotshot fighter pilot. Besides, you yourself may have gone through a similar experience before and ended up in a line of work different from what you originally planned, so it's only fair that you give your daughter the same flexibility as far as her future career is concerned.

In any case, you should teach your daughter that it's okay for her to go down a different path, whether by her own decision or because she ultimately did not become eligible for her original career choice. Raise her spirits further by telling her she could still make a name for herself in any other field for as long as she puts in enough time and hard work.

Help her develop a love for math and science

According to psychologist and parenting advice guru Dr. Sylvia Rimm and women's advocacy writer Sondra Forsyth (author of *Girls Seen and Heard: 52 Life Lessons for our Daughters*), among the essential traits that your daughter needs to develop is proficiency in science and mathematics.

It is no secret that a lot of people (not just children) abhor math and science because of the difficult assignments, the many principles that need to be learned, and the belief that it won't have much bearing in their later lives unless they work in jobs that clearly call for more than basic knowledge of these two subjects. However, these subjects can and will help prepare anyone for the future regardless of their chosen career path. Specifically, they help develop a person's mental capacity by getting the mind used to the idea of analyzing, solving problems, weighing options, and making informed decisions, which are some of the things we do every day, especially when we reach adulthood.

Bear in mind that this doesn't mean your daughter should become the best student in those two subjects in her class at all costs. What it simply states is that she needs to develop a love for those two subjects to the point that she learns to embrace challenging situations instead of avoiding them.

You may want to consider signing her up for supplementary math and science learning workshops. You may also expand your existing home library to include math and science books and magazines that can further enrich her knowledge. Whenever she has free time at home after having done her homework and her share of the chores, why not encourage her to play educational games that help reinforce her observational, analytical, and problem-solving skills? As she gets older, she can take on more challenging games as a form of recreation.

Also, you should try to make this additional learning a part of your daughter's everyday routine while still providing her with other opportunities for her to further develop herself (i.e. by reinforcing her self-esteem, by making new friends, etc.). Even if she is doing exceptionally well in those subjects, it wouldn't hurt to give her an even bigger edge that will certainly be useful to her in her later years.

Chapter 6. Protecting Your Daughter from Predators

Predators in this sense are males (typically older adult men but some young teenaged males as well) who prey on young girls for reasons that are sexual or financial in nature (sometimes even both). Obviously, such twisted individuals have no place in society, yet their number seems to grow by the day and they continue to succeed in luring unsuspecting children into situations that would have lasting negative effects on both body and mind.

You probably already know that these pieces of filth live in the same world that we do but you really didn't give them much thought. However, once you consider the possibility that even your own daughter could easily become a victim of any of these individuals, you will realize why this recurring problem should concern you as well.

As parents, we are responsible for protecting our daughters (and our sons) from these individuals who have no remorse harboring—and indulging in—their perverted fantasies. Our daughters have every right to live happy, healthy childhoods wherein they are free to grow up and learn more about themselves and the world around them. They should never have to live their lives in fear of these people and the worst that they can possibly do.

No parent in their right mind would expect their young daughter to know on her own how to effectively deal with situations that will put her safety at great risk. Your little girl will always count on you to protect her from harm and to show her the right way. Furthermore, it's not enough to rely only on law enforcement at all levels and on the state and federal criminal justice systems to deter people with less than noble intentions from preying on vulnerable children. Parents need to be more proactive in guaranteeing their daughters' safety and in teaching them how to avoid people who could hurt them physically, emotionally, or both.

Here are some helpful tips on how you can ensure your daughter is better protected against predators.

If a person makes her feel uncomfortable, she should immediately avoid them

In your daughter's regular interactions outside the home, such as in school, it is inevitable for her to come into contact with adults. As much as you would want to have faith that teachers, school officials, your neighbors, and other kids' parents are every bit as concerned about your daughter's well-being as you are, the times we live in can make it difficult for you to assume that that would be true in every single case. Thus, it would be much better for you to find out as much as you can about these and other adults whom your daughter interacts with regularly. You also need to know if there is anything about them that she doesn't like. If she says that someone among them makes her feel uncomfortable, drop everything and let her tell you all that she can about that person.

You could try to teach your daughter about the telltale signs that a person is a sexual predator. Unfortunately, many of these individuals have become highly skilled at adopting seemingly harmless personas that they can easily avoid suspicion for the longest time, and so their true intentions remain unknown to others until it is too late. You can thus simply tell your daughter to be more alert the minute she starts feeling uncomfortable in a particular individual's presence and to tell you or any trusted adult at the first opportunity about her unpleasant experience even if there has been no bodily contact.

In cases like this, you should remind your daughter to avoid that person from now on (or if she can't completely avoid that person, to make sure she is in the company of a trusted adult whenever that person interacts with her). Even interaction with the person in the form of phone conversations and exchanges of text messages need to be avoided. It would be much better for her to err on the side of caution than to allow herself to be lured into a potentially risky situation simply because she would not want to hurt another person's feelings by ignoring them. Remember, there's no point in your daughter being concerned about another person's feelings and in being kind to them if there is enough evidence that they have no concern at all for her by making her feel uncomfortable.

It also goes without saying that you should teach your daughter to minimize her interactions with random strangers and to instead stay within her own social circle that includes those people with whom she is already familiar. She still has to try to be kind even to strangers, at least until she feels she has enough reasons to put her own safety above others' by avoiding them.

It's okay to make a scene when absolutely necessary

If your daughter can't get out of a potentially risky situation with a suspected predator by simply avoiding them, then she should at least try to draw enough attention to herself to dissuade any would-be predator from doing anything at all to her—even simply talking to her—right then and there. Often, even just the possibility that other people will notice right away will discourage a predator from interacting any further with his intended victim.

You should teach your daughter that making a scene is acceptable in this case as it could easily get people's attention, including the attention of people who are in a position to do something to successfully resolve the situation in case it escalates such as a teacher, a police officer, or any other well-meaning adult. Thus, she should not hesitate to scream, start bawling uncontrollably, throw a tantrum—anything that could easily get anyone to look in her direction.

Help her come up with an escape plan

This step is more applicable when your daughter is old enough to commit lengthy, detailed instructions to memory. This means you should help her devise detailed step-by-step instructions for her to follow should she find herself in the company of a predator and there's no one nearby who could come to her rescue.

What should she do if she is at school and a male teacher corners her in the hallway and starts asking her seemingly inappropriate questions about her appearance? Or how about if she is at a party at a classmate's house and one of her male friends starts touching her where she doesn't want to be touched? You should work together with your daughter in thinking of possible scenarios as well as what she should do in each one. There should also be a list of contact numbers of people she could call on for help depending on where she is and what is happening around her (Of course, dialing 911 will always be an option in many cases.).

The only drawback here is you won't be able to cover every possible scenario because you can't really predict which situations your daughter will face, as well as what potential predators will do next. Still, taking this valuable step in ensuring her safety will make her better prepared in facing different situations on her own, especially those with even the slightest possibility of her coming in direct contact with anyone who means to do her harm.

Find out if there are any registered sex offenders in your community

Municipal, state, and federal law enforcement agencies throughout the country have continually growing databases of those who have been found guilty of crimes that are sexual in nature. This number also includes those who are out on parole to determine if they are worthy of being allowed to join the rest of society and live once more as free citizens.

If you have a hunch that someone you know could be a convicted sex offender on parole, then it might be best to find out if they have any record in the US Department of Justice's National Sex Offender Public Website (https://www.nsopw.gov/). This database includes registries in all 50 states, the District of Columbia, US territories, and Native

American tribes. If a person you wish to know more about happens to turn up in your search through the site, then the logical thing to do would be to tell your daughter to avoid them completely, whether they are her teacher, a neighbor, or even someone she looks up to. With about 75 percent of victims of sexual abuse reporting that they have had frequent prior nonsexual interactions with those who abused them, you should definitely intervene as soon as possible instead of giving the other person the benefit of the doubt and risk having your daughter become another statistic.

Of course, the database is not comprehensive enough to include *all* convicted sex offenders residing in the country. Also, this list includes only convicted offenders, not those who have not yet been found guilty in court and certainly not those who have a greater tendency to become sex offenders themselves but have not yet committed any crime. Thus, in addition to teaching your daughter about how to look out for herself when you're not around, you should not hesitate to refer to this database whenever you have a nagging uneasy feeling about someone you know or have heard about.

Remember, there is no such thing as being too cautious when it comes to guaranteeing your daughter's safety from those who aren't even the least bit concerned about it. You should therefore take the necessary steps within the scope of the law towards that end.

Chapter 7. The Joy of Raising Daughters

Did that chapter title surprise you? You may find it strange that this book decided to end with a chapter that most people would deem to be more appropriate at the beginning. After all, wouldn't it make much more sense to remind parents of the good things they can expect from raising daughters *before* they actually get started on it?

The truth is it doesn't really matter at which point in time that parents are reminded of the joy they could experience as they go about continually molding their curious, uncertain young girls into the intelligent, confident, and hardworking women of tomorrow. The important thing is that they eventually experience this joy by loving their daughters unconditionally and by being totally committed to their responsibility in raising them, even if they are reluctant to do so at first.

Besides, no written detailed description in a book about parenting can ever adequately describe the feeling of satisfaction of parents who have spent some of the best years of their lives loving and nurturing their little princess.

But in case you're still having doubts, probably because you're still getting the hang of it, this chapter will give you a rundown of some of the positive changes that having a daughter will bring into your life.

You will have no problem putting yourself second

As a working professional, you most likely already know that you have plenty of commitments as well as the need to fulfill all of them. You then come up with schedules and practice proper time management so that everything will run like clockwork, hence allowing you to achieve all your goals while ensuring efficient use of your available resources. All that, however, will go flying out the window the minute you welcome your baby girl into your life.

Do you have to get up early for work in the morning? Well, then, you can forget about it when your little girl starts crying and wakes you up in the middle of the night for a diaper change. Are you planning on pulling an all-nighter finishing that big report you have to submit the following day? Be ready to drop everything and leave your laptop and presentation materials in the corner the moment your precious sugar plum runs up to you and asks you to check whether there are any monsters hiding under her bed or in her closet. Are you scheduled to meet with an important prospect who has given you no more than an hour to try to talk him into buying what you sell? Guess what; your sweet darling princess has just become your only priority when you found out she has come down with chicken pox.

It goes without saying that it's always a new reason every time, and the time of day when your little girl says she needs you will always be different. She doesn't care, nor does she even *know*, that by crying out for you and by your coming to her rescue, you could easily lose some much-needed rest, risk missing out on an important career-enhancing opportunity, or fail to secure a lucrative business deal that could have assured you of financial security for the rest of your life. However, any sensible parent will tell you that it's much more preferable for them to give up all that than to not provide their daughters (and their sons) the one thing they need the most during their formative years—their time.

You will always come across opportunities to get promoted or make more money (It just takes a keen eye to be able to spot such opportunities as they won't always appear obvious.), but you have only one chance to watch your daughter grow up during her formative years and to provide her all the love and care she needs before she becomes ready to stand up on her own. If you know what you will gain from getting directly involved during this stage of her life, you will not mind missing out on more than a few opportunities for professional growth.

You are reminded to truly enjoy even the simple things in life

While she's still little, try taking your daughter out for a trip to the park, the grocery store, the library, or any other establishment or landmark within walking distance of your home. You will notice on your way to wherever it is you're going that you will stop several times for about as many different reasons.

This is not because you've encountered any problems, though. On the contrary, it's because your little girl will keep interrupting your walk towards your intended destination so that she can pay closer attention to just about anything that captures her interest, including things she hasn't seen before. It could be a shamrock, a maple tree showing the first signs of autumn, a clear blue noontime sky devoid of clouds, or even just a shiny quarter sticking out like a sore thumb on the sidewalk. She knows that the two of you have someplace to go to, but she can't help it. She feels she needs to stop whatever she's doing so that she can truly admire things that may seem trivial to you but are nonetheless fascinating to her.

Your daughter is probably still too young to know the meaning behind the popular expression "stop and smell the roses," and yet that is precisely what she is doing whenever she temporarily forgets about her main goal to devote some of her time and energy to indulge in small things that nonetheless give her joy (or at least, satisfy her curiosity). Perhaps that is one thing you didn't realize you've been missing out on all this time. You may have important goals that you need to fulfill, whether long-term or short-term, but no one ever said that the only thing you are allowed to do is to work towards fulfilling those goals. You should thus find time for other important things such as your family, your passions, and even yourself.

Give yourself temporary breaks from your job, your business, or whatever it is you do for a living so that you will have time for the other things you've always wanted to do. Whether it's going on a weekend vacation with your family, pursuing a hobby you've had since childhood, doing volunteer work, or even just taking your kids with you to the ice cream parlor on Saturday afternoons.

For fathers: You learn to let your heart speak again

If you're a father, you may have been brought up to believe that you needed to be strong in both mind and body in order to successfully take on any challenge you faced. Over time, you learned to embrace discipline, efficiency, and doing things according to plan that you became convinced that you needed to live the rest of your life with laser-like focus on your goals as well as nerves of steel just so you will survive. However, you may be surprised to know that having a daughter can permanently change your perspective.

You come to understand that spontaneity isn't always a bad thing when you smile upon seeing your laptop suddenly covered in sticky notes that have her doodles and drawings on them. You concede that the "soft approach" can sometimes work when you realize that her mere presence alone is usually all it takes for her to get you to stop whatever you're doing (no matter how important it is) and give her your attention.

And perhaps more importantly, you learn that the best solution doesn't always involve comprehensive planning, a wealth of resources, or the ability to improvise on the spot. Sometimes, a nice, warm hug can make anyone feel that, even for a few minutes, all their problems just seem to go away, whether it's you giving your little girl a hug or the other way around.

In a nutshell, a father should let his heart rather than his mind be his main guide. Raising daughters is indeed a challenging endeavor, but no problem is too difficult for any parent who listens to their heart more than their mind.

Conclusion

I hope this book was able to show you that raising girls can be a worthwhile and enjoyable endeavor, especially if you do it right by listening to your heart and having your daughter serve as your biggest inspiration to be a good parent.

The next step is to apply what you have learned from reading this book and to spend every day of the next few years making sure your daughter has the things she needs—confidence, a good education, an assurance of safety, and, most importantly, *your time.*

Remember to enjoy every step you take with her on that exciting journey of molding her into a princess with a kind heart and a warrior with the will to persevere until she achieves her goals.

Thank you and good luck!

Raising
Teenagers

How to Raise Teenagers
into Balanced and
Responsible Adults in
Today's Cluttered World
through Positive
Parenting

Introduction

Have you wondered if you're making the right decisions when it comes to raising your teenagers? Over the last years, there has been a lot of confusion about the role of boys and girls in our society. It's easy to see why parents are left with lots of unanswered questions when they're raising their children.

The teenage years constitute a period of great change for any person, and not just in terms of their age and their anatomy. In fact, the transition from pre-teenhood to teenhood has reportedly been taking many parents by surprise as they feel their children who were once harmless and precious little angels always clinging to mommy and daddy for protection seem to have transformed into fearless, unbridled wild animals with appetites to match (Of course, that particular description doesn't apply to all teenagers, but the transformation is no less obvious even among those who do not fit the stereotype!).

The fact remains, though, that teenagers are not yet adults even though they may seem far older and more aware of their surroundings compared to how they were before. Thus, they still need to be guided into making the right decisions for themselves, and no one is better qualified to help them in this regard than their own parents.

This book was written with the aim of educating parents on ensuring their teenaged children are better equipped to face the world as they become more independent. Although teenagers will inevitably have to manage on their own after they reach adulthood, parents are still given a few valuable years prior to that stage so that they can help their children gain a better understanding of themselves, the world around them, and the roles they need to fulfill.

This book will help parents teach their teenagers about how to adequately deal with various aspects of life while still allowing them to enjoy this period of major transformation. After all, what parent wouldn't want their children to have as much fun as they can (within the limits of decency, of course) in those precious remaining years before they face realities such as paying the bills, making important career decisions, and even raising families of their own?

The information herein is offered for informational purposes solely, and is universal as so. The presentation of the information is without contract or any type of guarantee assurance.

The trademarks that are used are without any consent, and the publication of the trademark is without permission or backing by the trademark owner. All trademarks and brands within this book are for clarifying purposes only and are the owned by the owners themselves, not affiliated with this document.

Chapter 1. Teenagers Need Guidance, Too

Middle school, high school, sleepovers, house parties, crushes, heartbreak, coming home late at night (sometimes even in the wee hours of the morning)—these are just some of the many things that you will witness almost every day as a parent of a teenaged child. In other words, the teenage years are an exciting period for both children and their parents partly because of the greater number of possibilities compared to what was prevalent during early childhood. Parents of teens are thus fortunate to be able to play an active part in helping their children become more mature and responsible by the time they enter adulthood just a few short years away.

However, more possibilities also mean more opportunities for things to go wrong. With your children now capable of knowing and doing far more than when they were younger, you cannot simply allow them to decide for themselves and hope that they will know what they should do in every situation. You might think that every single bit of knowledge that you taught them in the past will still have some bearing in their later years. On the contrary, the situations they will regularly face during this time are not the same as those they regularly faced when they were younger such as being afraid of the dark, learning to ride a bike (and getting cuts and bruises in the process), and feeling sad and anxious whenever they are separated from you.

The fact remains that teenagers are still children who need to be guided into making the right decisions every time. By now, therefore, your main focus as a parent starts to shift from fulfilling your children's basic needs (i.e. food, clothing, shelter, nurturing, etc.) to teaching them about what they need to do in situations they will regularly encounter. The following are just some of those situations, which by themselves are also reasons enough for parents to take the idea of raising teenagers more seriously:

1. Because teenagers interact with the world outside more often and with greater independence from their parents, they are no longer completely shielded from people and situations that could negatively influence their way of thinking as well as their behavior. Their parents won't always be by their side to advise them not to pick up certain habits that run contrary to legal standards, ethical standards, or both. For example, your teens might incorrectly think it's

203

perfectly acceptable to express open hatred towards people of different race, skin color, or religious belief simply because they see other people getting away with it almost every day.

2. Another significant problem teens face today is that they risk getting involved with the wrong kinds of people to satisfy their need to belong to a group that will readily accept them. Belonging to certain social circles is one of the things that give teenagers confidence since they feel they have been accepted into a group that opens its doors to only a select few. However, the problem here is that not all groups that are willing to welcome them with open arms have their best interests in mind. Exposure to such individuals raises the possibility of teens committing acts that will put themselves on the

wrong side of the law, especially if they have no positive moral foundation to guide them in every decision they make. Isn't it alarming when you read the news and you come across a report about a burglary, an assault, or even an incident of rape or murder committed by someone who is not yet old enough to buy a beer?

3. Peer pressure could also lead teens to participate in non-violent activities that can nonetheless put themselves and other people at great risk. Issues such as underage alcohol drinking, cigarette smoking, and even abuse of controlled substances will pave the way to a whole host of health problems. Furthermore, being under the influence of alcohol, prohibited narcotics, and even prescription medicines can impair their

senses, their perception of reality, their judgment, and their self-control. Thus, they could end up hurting themselves and others.

4. Children are more susceptible to mental and emotional health issues during their teenage years than when they were younger. Because they begin to feel greater pressure to excel, to be accepted, and to conform to standards that seem to become more demanding over time, they can easily get overwhelmed by even the smallest things. Parents therefore always need to be on the lookout for signs that their teens are barely able to keep it together to prevent it from evolving into a much more debilitating condition. Otherwise, teenagers who are unable to overcome depression end up missing out on the best possible benefits

of their last few years before adulthood
instead of enjoying them.

The challenge is indeed great even for parents,
but they need not be too intimidated by it. As a
parent, you don't need to play it by ear. You
have your own experiences as a teenager to fall
back on whenever you feel you're at a loss.
However, if you're having trouble remembering
how your own parents raised you before, this
book will help refresh your memory as you live
each day of your children's teenage years
setting them straight and turning them into
model citizens.

Chapter 2. The Truth about Teenagers

Do you still know what's it like to be in a teenager's shoes? You may have difficulty remembering it after having been an adult for so long. The many responsibilities you needed to fulfill as an adult up to today have probably made it more and more difficult for you to recall exactly how you survived your teenage years to become the person you are now, so don't feel bad if the memories aren't as clear as you want them to be.

You are not alone in facing this problem. Many parents of teenagers are surprised at how much their own children had changed in just a few short years. They are surprised partly because they've forgotten what it was like to have gone through that same transformation themselves.

Perhaps a brief refresher will help you better understand teenagers and what makes them tick, so that you will know how to properly interact with them. As you read through this chapter, you may even begin to remember how your life was like when you were at that particular stage.

Teenagers are not as simple as you may think

Teenagers are not just lazy young people who spend more time on their mobile phones and tablets, listen to loud music, and hate the whole world (especially their parents). On the contrary, many of the people in that age group are actually fun-loving, intelligent, and excited (sometimes a bit too excited) to try a lot of new things.

As a parent, it is imperative that you do what is necessary to help your teenaged children further develop the positive attributes that make them special. It will be a long and difficult journey for both of you because, while you are helping them develop their potential, you are doing your best to figure them out yourself. However, you will realize all your efforts will have been worth it when you see your teens leading happy and successful lives now and in the future when they become adults.

They think they have everything all figured out

Having already left their early childhood behind, your teenagers will start getting rather confident—cocky even—that they know all everyone needs to know about life. As a parent, you of course know better, and so you still need to be there to enlighten them on how the world out there really is, particularly the truth that it won't always be sunshine and lollipops, and that it won't always make things easy for them. In any case, the human mind is believed to be fully mature only when a person reaches age 25, so you definitely know that your teens still have a long way to go as far as knowing everything is concerned.

They will want greater independence from you

Do you remember when your children still got all tearful and clingy during those first few times that you dropped them off at school? That separation anxiety will have fully eroded by the time they finally enter their teenage years. They will no longer be looking for mom or dad all the time to help them solve their problems or to simply just hug them tightly to reassure them that they are loved and accepted. They will begin wishing to be in the company of others, usually teens just like them, or to just be left alone.

Don't worry, though, as your teens know fully well that they still need to come home to you at the end of the day. It's just that they have now become old enough to know that there is a lot more to life than being with you all the time. Letting them get to know other people is crucial to their mental and emotional development, so you can't totally prevent them from going out into the world and establishing new relationships. Of course, you still need to remind them to be more discerning when it comes to choosing the company they keep (This will be discussed in detail in a later chapter.).

It's not just the physical separation that becomes increasingly evident here; the emotional separation between you and your teens starts to manifest itself during this period as well. Despite you and your teens living under the same roof and spending plenty of time at home together, there will be instances wherein they will be too preoccupied with something else (like chatting with their friends or playing video games) to even engage in conversation with you.

You'll find yourself still fussing over them

Your teenaged children's desire for greater independence from you partly stems from their wishing to be free from your constant watching over them and your being always at the ready to swoop in when they're in pain or in need of assistance.

You can't help it, though. Even when your children are no longer the adorable little munchkins you constantly chased after to make sure they didn't hurt themselves, part of you will still want to be always physically around them like a hawk. There really is nothing wrong with this because it is part of every parent's instinct, but if you want your teens to eventually discover their true potential and strength in overcoming difficulties, you need to be willing to let them trip and fall (both literally and figuratively) once in a while. It may be difficult for you at first, but the real magic happens when you sit back and watch, not when you're constantly participating directly in it.

You can still occasionally offer unsolicited guidance to your teens to help them find their inner strength. You just need to keep it in moderation lest you put them off through your constant fussing and make them want to spend time with you even less.

They will start voicing out their opinion

Your teenagers know more now than when they were younger partly because they have become more observant and critical of themselves and their surroundings. One of the things they are likely to do is to state what they have observed, as well as how it makes them feel.

The biggest drawback here is that not everything they say is pleasant to the ear. You probably already know now that teenagers are frequent whiners, which lends credence to the observation that they are still little kids who are simply older biologically. Sometimes they whine about things that are beyond their control, but there will also be times when they will whine about things that are *within* their control. In this case, you need to be patient with them and explain to them that there are more practical alternatives to whining. Gently but firmly remind them that the talents and the skills they possess can be put to good use in looking for solutions to some of the problems they keep complaining about all the time.

To understand why your teens are more vocal now than they ever were before, we move on to the next truth, which is...

They will always need someone who will listen

As someone who has been raising children for years, you most likely already know by now that your own offspring won't always be as vocal as you want them to be, especially when it comes to expressing their emotions. It could be because they're worried you might find their concerns to be amusing, trivial, or worse, not worth your time.

You need to dispel your teens' misconceptions as early as now by telling them that you are ready and willing to listen to them whenever they have something on their minds. Don't make them think that you are always too preoccupied doing something more important. Anything that has to do with your children is far more important than everything else in your life as a parent, and they need to be able to see this in your words and in your actions in order for them to believe you.

If you're willing to listen but they're not willing to talk just yet, you can simply tell them they can always come to you even if you're watching TV, reading the paper, or working in the garage. If they come to you telling you they have something rather serious on their minds (or even if it's a relatively mundane piece of news like the principal's car being the latest target of the school prankster), then you should drop everything and immediately lend an ear.

Show your teens that you are just as approachable as anyone else they know, perhaps even more so. You may be an authority figure to them, possibly even their biggest critic as well, but you can also be their most sympathetic supporter, and you start fulfilling this role by giving them the chance to be heard.

Half of the time, you're the villain in their story

Ironic as it may sound, parents who keep showering their teenaged children with their time, nurturing, and unconditional love can and will be regarded as nuisances. Teens sometimes can't help but feel that their own parents are on a mission to prevent them from having the time of their lives at the stage wherein they are beginning to enjoy much greater freedom than when they were younger. And it's not just you who is the villain in their eyes; virtually *every* adult they come across who tries to set them straight is, by default, a threat to their desire to have fun.

Remember that many of the ways of instilling discipline that you used on them when they were younger have a much greater likelihood of backfiring on you now that they are teens, so

219

don't assume it will be just as easy. Instead, you will have to adopt entirely new approaches to discourage them from behaving or acting improperly.

The temptation to retaliate in kind can be overwhelming, especially if your teenagers show no remorse for whatever hurtful things they've just said or done. However, you will not accomplish anything by simply giving in to your anger and frustration. Don't even try to engage them in a debate to convince them of why your duty as their parent will benefit them, lest you get tired of listening to and trying to answer every single one of their rebuttals.

You and your teens are not in a battle to establish one party's superiority over the other. Your authority as a parent will always be beyond debate, and that is why you don't need to come up with a riposte to every illogical claim they make about you being wrong about this or that from their point of view.

In any case, you need to make your teenagers see that you are on their side in the sense that you want to ensure they get what they need in order to become responsible adults, even if they won't always agree with you.

But through it all, they will always still need you

Teenagers are still children who need to be continually set straight. And just like younger children, teenagers also need love, acceptance, inspiration, and validation from the people who truly matter to them, not the least of which are their parents. They won't always say it, but it is what they need and thus, you should always be ready to provide it to them.

They may have grown up by a few years, but they are still the same little angels who need you to help them learn to be confident enough to face life on their own.

Chapter 3. Every Day with Your Teenagers

As with raising younger children, raising teenagers requires parents to make themselves available to their children as often as possible, preferably 24/7. As a parent, you cannot say that your work of raising your kids is done when they finally get the hang of such things as picking up after themselves, doing the chores without being prodded to do so, getting good grades in school, and not making a mess whenever they eat their meals or use the bathroom. In fact, by the time children enter their teen years, they are still a long way from finally being independent, and so they need to be continually guided until then.

This chapter discusses the key pointers you need know for each day that you will spend raising your teenagers so that they will become adults you can be proud of someday.

Continue being a role model to them

You led your children by example as you raised them during their younger years. However, just because they're a bit older now doesn't mean you may no longer require them to speak and act as you would, depending on the situation. In fact, they may need even more guidance from you at this stage since you are also starting to give them even more leeway.

Your interactions with your teens at home should also serve as opportunities for you to show them through your words and actions how you yourself deal with whatever comes your way. Keep exercising prudence and self-control, especially when you are faced with challenging situations. Also, you should try not to look discouraged if things get too difficult even for you. Remember, you are also teaching your teens to draw strength from within themselves, and you cannot accomplish this if they sense through your words and actions that you are on the verge of raising that white flag.

The last thing they need is a parent trying to be a friend

One mistake parents make is thinking they need to please their children all the time, especially when their children enter their teenage years. Many parents even incorrectly assume that their children want greater independence from them because they (parents) are no longer fun to be with. To counter this, these parents try desperately to connect with their teens on various levels, even going so far as giving their teens the freedom to do just about *anything* they want.

You don't need to go to great lengths just to get on your teens' good side, lest you risk giving them the impression that you are wanting for their attention, which will make them lose respect for you as their parent. Rather, it is your teens who need to get on your good side. It is your instructions that need to be followed, especially at home. It is your will and not theirs that matters more because your will is focused on caring for them and keeping them safe. Hence, you should be a guide and a disciplinarian who will set them along the right path, not an eager brown-noser who always encourages them to do as they please even if it could potentially bring harm to themselves and others.

In other words, you need to be a parent more than you need to be a friend to your teens.

Don't rely too much on books and magazines about parenting

This tip may seem strange (ironic even, as you are reading a book about parenting at this very moment). However, it simply reminds parents to place more faith in their own experience and instincts than in things that were written by people they hardly even know. The reality is all teenagers are unique; a specific set of guidelines might work in raising one child but not in raising another, not even a sibling.

Author and educator Robert Evans, EdD, states that there is another drawback to having more faith in parenting books than is necessary. Even if you've followed all the tips you've read, your relationship with your teenagers could end up no better than what it was before (especially if you don't spend enough time knowing what your teens really need from you), and this could lead to feelings of disappointment or a desire to overcompensate without first thinking things through.

The goal in reading such books is to gain a fresh new perspective on your children and their behavior, not to follow every piece of given advice to the letter. You should let these references serve as guides for you in figuring out the answers, instead of assuming that these will explicitly state to you every single action you need to take.

Harbor nothing but positive expectations

As proven in a study conducted by experts at Wake Forest University in North Carolina, it is important for you not to have any negative expectations at all about your teenagers. Otherwise, having only negative expectations could eventually bring about the realities that you as a parent fear the most. For example, you shouldn't constantly worry about your teenagers becoming addicted to controlled substances so as not to raise the likelihood of it ever happening.

You should instead make a habit out of hoping for only the best for your teens. Teach them to be prudent and confident in themselves so that you will be confident in them as well. You don't need to be specific in your expectations for them for as long as they are happy with and are benefiting from the decisions they make.

Make it mandatory for them to go offline every once in a while

Although it is in many ways beneficial, the proliferation of mobile electronic gadgets has also had a number of negative effects on children, even teenagers who have always been understood to have much greater self-control. Because they spend more and more time on their gadgets, teens could end up engaging less frequently in face-to-face interactions outside of school (i.e. with family and friends). Lack of interaction during this stage of life could hurt anyone's future prospects of ensuring genuine relationships (both professional and personal) that will last. It could also potentially lead to depression as the mind gradually begins to draw comfort from the perceived enjoyment provided by the gadgets more than it does from actual interactions with other people, including those who are genuinely concerned for the teen's welfare.

The obvious solution to this is to impose an "offline period" for your teens whenever you're together, whether at home or while you're traveling. During each offline period, they are not to use their gadgets (This also includes desktop and laptop computers and video gaming consoles.) for playing games, browsing their social media accounts, watching videos, chatting for hours on end with their friends, or any other unimportant activity that could eat up a lot of their time without their knowing it. Encourage them to find more practical means of recreation such as reading books, talking to you about how their day went, playing board games by themselves or with their younger siblings, or getting exercise outdoors.

Making offline time mandatory is one of the most effective ways you can show your teens that gadgets aren't prerequisites for truly enjoying life. Thus, you should implement it as often as possible.

If your instincts tell you something is wrong, they're probably right

Through the years, parents gradually develop a sort of sixth sense that picks up indicators of their children engaging—or even about to engage—in actions that can bring harm to themselves or others. Many say this sense comes from the parents' own experiences of being exposed to such actions (without necessarily actively participating in these) when they themselves were younger.

If this sixth sense of yours suddenly gets triggered, it might be best for you to pay heed to it instead of dismissing it as a false alarm. Remember, parents should not take certain things lightly, especially if it involves their children's well-being. Otherwise, taking the necessary action only much later can also mean taking action when it's already too late to be of any good.

For example, if you suspect your teenagers are involved in underage drinking or substance abuse, you should be on the lookout for signs such as noticeable unexplained changes in physical appearance, inconsistent behavior, frequent isolation from family and friends, and poor grades. Or if you have reason to believe your teens have become addicted to internet porn, find out exactly how much time they spend online and whether or not they keep to themselves far more often than they used to do.

When these or other indicators frequently manifest, have a talk with your teens to find out what's going on. Remember to tell them what you've noticed about them, not what you suspect they've been doing. Be patient and give your teens the opportunity to speak so that you will know why they engage in such activities. If they're not yet willing to talk about it, firmly insist that you want to hear their side, not give them a lengthy lecture as to why you feel that what they're doing is wrong. Once they've opened up and you've identified the reason, see if you and your teens can work towards a solution, either by avoiding the cause for the behavior or by offering healthier and more practical alternatives.

Throughout the process, you should make your teens aware that you are there to help them and not judge them. Show them that, even if you do not condone their actions, you will always sympathize with them because of your love for them being much greater than your dislike of their improper behavior. If you yourself had also engaged in such activities a few times when you were younger, you can share with them what you went through while also telling them how you were able to overcome those habits. Don't forget to mention that just because you engaged in it when you were younger doesn't mean you will allow them to go down that path, even if they tell you they will exercise the necessary self-control.

Harsh realities are inevitable, so don't shield your teenagers from those

Perhaps your teenagers became used to getting precisely what they wanted when they were much younger. The reality, however, is that things will not always proceed according to plan, and as they get older, they will more regularly experience unpleasant situations such as failure, disappointment, regret, and heartbreak.

You of course would want to protect your teenagers from anything that could weaken their spirit, but you will actually be hindering their emotional growth by doing so. Letting them experience harsh realities early on is sometimes necessary as it provides them opportunities to reach deep within themselves and discover the strength they need to bounce back from those unpleasant events.

Whether it's your son beating himself up over not making the football team at school or your daughter crying her eyes out because the "mean girls" in school humiliated her in front of everybody, you shouldn't try to take your teens' focus away from the reason for their pain. Instead, you will have to help them look for the strength they need, especially during the first few times since they will still be at a loss as to what they should do. Eventually, however, they should learn to accomplish it on their own because they won't always have you to guide them in this, especially when they become adults.

Get to know their friends

One way of knowing your teens' beliefs and preferences is finding out the company they usually keep. What do their friends usually do for fun? How are their respective families and home environments? How are they performing in school? By answering these questions, your teens can give you a glimpse of who their friends are, as well as whether or not they could serve as positive influences for your teens.

As your teens go out in the world and make new friends, it is inevitable that they will come across similarly-aged people who have negative reputations whether through their own admission, physical evidence of their actions, or simply hearsay. If your teens happen to mention regular interactions with such individuals, it is important that you do not immediately express your disapproval of those whom they have chosen as their friends even if your instinct tells you to do otherwise. Let this instead prompt you to watch your teens' behavior more closely. If they start regularly exhibiting negative behaviors (i.e. swearing, poor grades, lack of respect for others, etc.) following their regular interactions with certain friends, you can then finally intervene and instruct them to avoid those people from that point on.

In any case, you should make your teens aware that you trust them to choose their acquaintances wisely and that they know how to look out for themselves. You can't choose their friends for them, but you can advise them on the kinds of people whom they should *not* choose to be their friends.

For your peace of mind, you may even want to invite your teens' friends over at your home to see them face-to-face and to know firsthand how they behave in the company of others. You can probably organize a weekend movie marathon or video game night (Just make sure the films and games are age-appropriate.) or even an after-school study session (for as long as it doesn't end too late) to encourage their friends to come over without giving them the impression that they will be there simply to undergo your scrutiny.

You can then ask your teens' friends to share a little about themselves during their first visit and then discreetly observe their interactions with your teens on subsequent visits. This way, you will get to see for yourself if your teens have indeed chosen peers who truly look out for them or if they have become involved with people who could mean trouble with a capital T.

Remind them of the importance of accepting others

People often fear what they do not understand, and teenagers are guilty of this as well. This is partly because teenagers will still have that childhood tendency to believe what is presented to them without first verifying the facts. As such, there is a possibility of your teens mimicking some of the people around them for no reason other than "Everybody else is doing the same thing."

This is often the case in instances of discrimination. With all the hate circulating in our society, your teens need to do far more than simply keep quiet about it, or worse, accept as truth any negative perceptions of others based simply on their physical attributes (i.e. skin color, gender, whether or not they have bodily defects, etc.), their culture and heritage, their religious beliefs, or even their political affiliations. Otherwise, they could get easily swayed and begin to harbor wildly inaccurate opinions that could hurt their chances of establishing and maintaining relationships in various settings.

First of all, you need to encourage your teens to pick up the habit of doing adequate research before formulating their own conclusions. You should also remind them that everyone deserves equal opportunities in school, work, and other endeavors and that no one deserves to be discriminated against simply for being different.

Ask your teens how they would feel if they were in these other people's shoes in order for them to put their minds at work. Give them a sense of how those people feel whenever they are the subject of unjust scrutiny by those who choose to remain ignorant. Once your teens realize the difficulty such people face, they will learn to sympathize with them even more.

Furthermore, you need to set an example for them through the way you interact with your neighbors, your coworkers, and even random people you meet on the street. Show them that being friendly and courteous towards everyone instead of being prejudiced is the normal thing—and the right thing—to do.

Be a gardener in raising your teens

It's probably safe to assume you know even a little about gardening. When raising plants, you do not arrange their leaves, their stems, and all their other parts a certain way to ensure their growth. Instead, you simply make sure they get adequate nutrients from the soil, water, and sunlight and that they are protected from unwanted company such as pests. For as long as you continue to provide your plants with the necessary nutrients and security, they will grow up strong and healthy, and they will truly be a sight to behold.

It may help you if you raise your teenagers the same way. Much of the work you do as a parent will go into ensuring that your teens have the necessary knowledge and upbringing that will enable them to deal with everyday situations by themselves. There's no need for you to be where they are all the time to tell them what they should do, especially if you have been able to instill in them a sense of responsibility and confidence through your interactions at home.

Bonus tip: Come up with contingency plans

One of the realities that parents of teenagers face is the fact that their children will spend *a lot* of time out of the house. Specifically, many teenagers spend more time out of the house than what their parents would want. This means that, half of the time, parents are unaware of the exact situations their teens face—unless, of course, they are able to contact them immediately via mobile phone.

But what if, for some reason, your teens are unable to contact you immediately and vice-versa? Much as you would want to, you cannot be there all the time to advise them on how to act, and this is partly because you want to give them greater independence as they get older. Nonetheless, just like any other sensible parent, you would want your children to be better equipped with what they need so that they would remain in one piece at the end of each day even with all the nasty stuff the world will throw at them.

You can help your teens in this regard by formulating basic step-by-step plans on what they need to do during worst-case scenarios. For example, what should your teenaged son do if he's about to go back home from a friend's house in the middle of the night while you and your spouse happen to be out of town and he has no car available? Whom should your teenaged daughter ask for help if she is at a party and one of her male friends can't seem to keep his hands off her after having had a little too much to drink? Try to think of as many hypothetical scenarios as you can and plan together with your teens so that they will already know what each plan entails instead of being told about it only at the last minute.

Coming up with detailed contingency plans will be time-consuming and may even prove unnecessary, especially if your teenagers completely avoid people and situations that will put their safety as well as those of others at risk. Still, it's far better to have such plans in place and not need them than to need them but not have them.

Chapter 4. Disciplining Your Teenagers

It was discussed in an earlier chapter that teenagers still need guidance just like how it was when they were younger. Guidance also encompasses discipline as a way of correcting improper behavior whenever necessary in the hope of raising teenagers who will be able to know right from wrong even without anyone telling them so every time.

Remember that discipline is more than just imposing physical punishment to discourage your teens from engaging in improper behavior. Besides, the use of spanking and other forms of corporal punishment on teenagers is frowned upon in many societies partly because teenagers are believed to be already in that stage wherein verbal rather than physical means of disciplining them are enough to get the message across. With that in mind, this chapter will talk more about how discipline should be implemented instead of which kinds of punishment are recommended.

Don't hesitate to reprimand them, especially if there is a need to do so

Most parents make the mistake of avoiding conflict by not disciplining their teenagers even if it is warranted for fear of being pushed away even further. Others break down and panic from not knowing what to do when their chosen approach to discipline doesn't seem to work on their teens.

Either way, you need to be firm whenever you decide to call your teens out for improper behavior or for not taking responsibility for their actions. Even if you have a feeling the unwanted actions will repeat themselves, you should not give up and think that there's no point in telling your teens again and again why some of the things they've been doing are wrong.

You may need to keep calling them out for their actions and imposing the necessary consequences (like no nighttime parties with friends or no video games for a week) more than a few times. The key here is for you to be consistent in order for your teens to get the message that you are dead serious about wanting them to act and behave as they should even if you're not around.

It is also important that you strike the right balance when disciplining your teens. If you become excessive in terms of punishment and consequences (such as laying your hands on

them or using hurtful language), you risk
making your teens fearful instead of respectful
of authority. If you fail to implement the
appropriate punishment for every time an
infraction is committed—or even refuse to
discipline them at all—you will end up with
teens who regard the idea of authority as
nothing but a joke.

Set the appropriate consequences for disobedience

This is actually a milder way of saying "make
the punishment fit the crime." This simply
means the punishment for a certain infraction
will not only be fair to both you and your teens
but will also get them to reflect on their own
about why what they did is wrong. For the first
time an offense is committed, you need to
calmly and clearly explain why it warrants

251

punishment as well as stress that any repeat instances of it are unacceptable.

When setting punishment, remember that you will only temporarily deprive your teens of certain *privileges* like quality time with their friends or opportunities for recreation doing some of the things they love. Under no circumstances should you deprive your children of any of their *rights* such as nourishment, shelter, clothing, or rest and sleep as a means of punishing them for their disobedience. They can last a day without certain privileges, but they certainly cannot last a day without the basic rights which every single person should have.

Choose your battles

Teenagers sometimes get too tired or too preoccupied with other things that they forget to follow even basic house rules (like not leaving their clothes in a messy heap in one corner of their room after they get home from school). Other times, they would deliberately refuse to follow your instructions. It would therefore seem almost natural for you to immediately hit the roof, especially after you've spent years drilling into their minds the need for obedience. However, even without them telling it to you, you need to at least try to understand their condition before you do anything else. In other words, you do not have to get all worked up every time your teenagers do something contrary to what is expected of them.

Choosing your battles in this context means knowing when you should intervene to remind or correct them and knowing when you need to hold back. To know if you should intervene or not, you need to find out first why your teens are acting the way they are, especially if it is not normal for them to be doing so. Maybe they're having a tough time in school, or it could be because they aren't feeling well.

No matter how their apparent unacceptable behavior manifests itself, you need to first know what the reason is as well as show them that you are genuinely concerned by letting them talk to you about what's bothering them (And as stated in the previous tip, you still have to stress why such behavior is unacceptable.). Remember, you have a much better chance of attracting flies with honey than with vinegar.

It's okay when you reprimand them for blatant acts of disobedience, but for harmless instances of self-expression that just happen to go against your standards or anyone else's, it would not be wise for you to call them out for it, much less berate them. For example, you may scold them for getting behind the wheel after having had a little too much to drink or for not taking out the garbage even after having reminded them several times, but not for dyeing their hair in loud colors or intentionally wearing mismatched socks when visiting Grandma.

Otherwise, if you opt to reprimand your teens for every single infraction they commit, they will realize over time that you do not plan on giving them any real freedom to explore the world and try new things on their own (as well as face the consequences of their decisions without being shielded by anyone). You will also risk making them even more afraid to think and act for themselves (since they feel that *everything* has to pass your scrutiny before they engage in it, which is obviously not always possible).

You should scold your teens if necessary, but you should also be willing to give them a break every now and then. Let them practice the important trait of discernment, of being able to first ask themselves if what they're about to do is right or wrong before they actually do it.

Talk it over with your spouse

Unless you're a single parent with sole custody of your teenagers, you need to discuss first with your spouse what your plans are on how to instill discipline. You need to work together and to come up with a plan that both of you will have no trouble implementing on your own or together. It is imperative for the two of you to be on the same page so that even if one of you is not around, the other can go about disciplining your teens whenever necessary without considerable deviations from the agreed-upon protocol, especially when choosing and implementing the appropriate punishment.

As with the first tip discussed in this chapter, the key here is consistency. Keep in mind that your teens are much smarter now than when they were younger. If they see that you and your spouse have differing views and preferences when it comes to discipline, they could use that to their advantage. For example, if they see that one of their parents is not as committed as the other is when it comes to punishing a certain infraction, they might appeal to that parent's sympathy and try to talk their way out of being punished.

You and your spouse need to be equally committed in making sure your teens walk along the right path, and you start by having a plan of action that both of you will understand.

Chapter 5. Helping Your Teenagers Prepare for the Future

As early as their high school years, your teenagers should already have plans as to what they want to do for the long term after they graduate. This chapter will discuss how you can help them come up with their own plans.

It wouldn't hurt to promote your preferred options

For any sensible parent, there are only two acceptable options after high school: continued education (i.e. college or trade/vocational schools) or legitimate employment.

You should discourage your teenagers from staying idle in the years after high school even if they don't feel like continuing their education just yet. They become old enough to land even just a part-time job during their high school years, and the post-high school period certainly will provide them with plenty of full-time job options that don't necessarily require a college education. Some of those jobs can even lead to long and rewarding careers with reasonable pay and other benefits, like in the case of "lifers"— military personnel who willingly spent most of their adult years in service beginning from their time in the enlisted ranks.

In any case, you need to encourage your teens to be productive during the time they are still figuring out what they really want to do for the long term. Also, there really is no timetable that they need to follow here, but they have a much better chance of securing the right long-term prospects (both education-wise and career-wise) if they come to a decision in the immediate post-high school period.

Don't force them into choosing and sticking to a specific path

Even if your teenagers have detailed plans for their future that don't seem to coincide with your expectations, you shouldn't immediately dismiss those plans. Don't worry for nothing is yet permanent by this time, and your children are still likely to change their minds later on after they have thought things through (and they may end up changing their minds more than once).

Furthermore, you should remind your teens that having a plan in place much earlier doesn't mean they need to stick to it at all costs. Their plan will simply serve as a guide for them in choosing the schools they want to go to or the jobs they want to apply for, which also includes any temporary jobs they may want to try before they finally become eligible for that which they really want to do.

Give them a chance to explore

If your teens want to pursue something worthwhile after they graduate from high school, but they're not yet sure what it is, it may be advisable to give them the opportunity to think about it long and hard well before that time finally comes.

You can help them decide by asking them what their favorite school subjects are, what their biggest aspirations are, or how they would like to help other people. They can then think of possible options based on what their answers will be to these and other related questions. Let them write down all the positives and negatives of each option and then narrow down their list to the two or three most viable choices.

You and your teens should know that this exercise is not meant to determine the exact career path they will eventually take. Rather, this is intended to help them orient their focus so that they will have a clearer idea of what they might want to do once they're old enough. They will become more motivated to prepare for the future if they have something specific to aim for, even if it is not yet definite.

Remind them that things won't always go according to plan

Your teens should also know early on that what they plan to achieve in the future might not become reality. Even with all their years of preparation and hard work, there's still a chance they would end up doing something that they didn't originally aspire for when they were younger. They will of course be disappointed when they realize for the first time that they are being led down an entirely different path.

You need to reassure them that 1) it is not necessarily anyone's fault—least of all theirs—if they end up differently from what they originally planned and 2) this sort of thing happens all the time. They will also come to a fork in the road by then, and so they will need to decide for themselves whether to set a new career goal or to continue along the present course and see where it takes them. They can prepare for this possible scenario in the present by having a plan B so they will know what they should do if plan A doesn't work for them. And if plan B doesn't work, they should have a plan C, and so on down the line. After all, being overprepared is much better than the alternative.

You may also want to share with them the true story of Jimmy the peanut farmer from Georgia. Jimmy was a young navy officer who had a promising career ahead of him. He had in fact planned on someday becoming Chief of Naval Operations, which was the highest possible position in the US Navy, and so he chose a career path that would bring him repeated promotions and choice assignments in the years that follow.

However, tragedy dashed all his hopes of advancing through the ranks. Shortly after his father had died, Jimmy was urged by his family to leave active duty in the navy earlier than planned so that he could take over his late father's peanut farming business. You may think that going from navy officer to peanut farmer was an unusual career move for anyone, but Jimmy essentially had no choice. He was of course disappointed at first because he had not planned for this (He, his wife Rosalynn, and their children had to give up their government-issued house and a number of other perks that came with his job.), but he graciously took what life had given him and he kept doing his best in the years since then.

One could say Jimmy was ultimately rewarded for his decision to leave the navy earlier than planned because of his having attained a renowned position that was even more prestigious than that of Chief of Naval Operations. He became a prominent member of the community upon his return to his home state of Georgia. Entering politics ten years after he left active duty, he served as a Georgia State Senator and then as Governor. And in 1977, twenty-three years after he was honorably discharged from active duty, the young navy officer who left behind a promising career and a life of adventure to take on the less glamorous job of running a peanut farm was sworn in as the thirty-ninth President of the United States. Of course, the man is none other than Jimmy Carter.

By telling your teens about Jimmy Carter's example, you teach them that things not going according to plan can sometimes lead to something much greater, so there's no reason for them to get discouraged every time that happens. They can treat every setback either as a learning experience or a step towards something even better than what they imagined (As their parent, you are likely to have experienced more than a few such instances yourself.). You could even tell them that the word "setback" is actually the shortened form of "setting up for a comeback" to further raise their spirits.

And who knows, one of your teens might even become President someday, too!

Chapter 6. Helping Your Teenagers Deal with Depression

The moodiness that you saw in your children when they were younger will likely once again manifest itself at various times throughout their teenage years. There will be noticeable differences, though, not the least of which is the possibility that what your teens will face will be far more debilitating than what they used to endure.

As a parent, you have every reason to be concerned about your teens' mental and emotional health, especially in view of teenaged depression being more common now than what it was before and of the growing number of people who have committed suicide without ever living through to adulthood. In fact, recent studies have ranked suicide as the second leading cause of death (next to accidents) among teenagers in the United States. Hence, the need to help teens successfully deal with depression and other mental health issues becomes paramount.

Even if you feel you have taken every possible precaution from the time your children were born, it is best for you not to leave anything to chance. You may need to take additional steps in making sure your teens can overcome depression and live with sound minds and happy, healthy hearts. It also goes without saying that your love, understanding, and support for your teens will go a long way in helping them stay on the road to recovery.

Depression versus anxiety

Anxiety is not the same as depression, although the former has often been said to pave the way for the latter, especially if it is left unchecked. Whereas anxiety is often an irrational fear of or aversion towards seemingly normal situations, depression is a more prolonged and more persistent feeling of sadness. This sadness becomes so great that the individual suffering from it ceases to function as they normally would. They begin to lack enthusiasm in everything they do, and they easily get agitated by things that didn't bother them as easily before.

Knowing the signs

You've probably often experienced having your younger children run to you crying while you're in the middle of doing something else and, even without your prodding, tell you a rather lengthy story about why they're sad or upset. However, it is not likely that your teens will come up to you and openly tell you they feel they're coming down with depression. As a parent, you will need to be aware of some telltale signs that your teens are already suffering from depression or even if they're simply on the verge of it.

- Prolonged bouts of inexplicable sadness
- A persistent feeling of emptiness, worthlessness, or guilt
- Low self-esteem
- Poor performance in school
- Inconsistent sleeping habits (i.e. sleeping too much or too little)
- Significant weight gain or loss over just a short period
- Increased irritability
- Frequent use of alcohol or drugs

- Dwelling on past failures and disappointments for longer than a few days
- Loss of interest in spending time with family and friends
- Loss of interest in activities from which they usually derived enjoyment (i.e. sports, music, etc.)
- Difficulty in concentrating and remembering things
- Apparent apathy even towards loved ones
- Frequent exhaustion
- Frequent complaints of pain and fatigue
- Expecting a bleak future for themselves
- Expressing intent to commit crime
- Thoughts of death and suicide

It may be easy to dismiss it if only one of the above signs is evident. However, it would do your teens a world of good if you already regard even just one manifestation as a cause for concern. You stand a better chance of preventing depression from gaining a foothold in your teens by having a watchful eye and a willingness to dig deeper even if things still appear to be "normal." Although recent studies show that only one out of eight teenagers today suffer from depression, it would be foolish to immediately assume that your children are among the remaining seven.

Insisting on finding out exactly what's going on may at first cause your teens to tighten up and refuse to talk about it, so you have to reiterate that you are doing this because you don't want what's troubling them to interfere with their day-to-day lives. Your persistence in this regard will gradually make them realize that they can talk to you about it anytime. This will in turn encourage them to be more open about their emotions when talking to other people they can also trust, especially their doctor.

Identifying the causes

Teenage depression is often caused by the following:

- Biological issues such as hormonal imbalance and impairment of the neurotransmitters in the brain
- Past experiences such as traumatic childhood memories (like the death of a loved one) and instances of physical and emotional abuse
- Inheritance of the condition from family members who also suffer from it
- Learned patterns of thinking wherein the child simply resigns themselves to

their fate instead of striving to come up
with solutions

- Present day challenges such as
  difficulties in their studies, being bullied,
  and problems at home

- Spending an unhealthy amount of time
  on social media (A study conducted in
  2014 revealed that teenage anxiety and
  depression were also linked to excessive
  social media usage.)

Consulting a doctor

Perhaps the biggest mistake you could make as
a parent is taking your teens' mental and
emotional health in your own hands. While it is
understandable that you would want your teens
to receive the best possible care, there are
instances wherein other people are more
qualified than you are in providing that care.

Fortunately, we have psychiatrists and other licensed mental health specialists who are the foremost experts when it comes to treating depression and other related conditions.

Indeed, even a parent who also happens to be a licensed psychiatrist with years of experience will be prudent enough to seek the unbiased second opinion of one of their peers so that they will be better aware of the true state of their children's mental health. Thus, you should be open to the idea of entrusting your teen's well-being to the right kind of expert.

You shouldn't wait until depression has already fully set in to finally have your teen see the appropriate specialists. This is because your teen has a better chance of recovering from the condition if they get the necessary professional help at the earliest possible time.

You should also discuss with their doctor what your plans are for supplemental treatment (This will be discussed later in this chapter.). Remember, it is important that you, your teens, and their doctor are all on the same page as far as treatment is concerned.

Primary treatment options

Your teen's doctor is the only individual who is authorized to prescribe treatment for depression. This treatment can be in the form of medicines, psychotherapy, or a combination of the two (which studies have proven to be far more effective than either medicines or psychotherapy administered exclusively). In more severe cases of depression, confinement in a hospital's psychiatric department may be required.

There is no one-size-fits-all treatment for teenage depression in view of the differences in personalities and behaviors among teens. The extent and the scope of the treatment will depend on factors including, but not limited to, the severity of the condition, the causes of the depression, and the home and school environments in which your teen regularly interacts. You are therefore discouraged from exploring possible primary treatment options on your own and instead learn to trust your teen's medical health professional. Whichever treatment is prescribed, you and your teen need to fully cooperate with the doctor's instructions as even just one lapse in treatment could greatly impede any progress made towards recovery.

Moreover, any treatment for your teen's depression is likely to be for the long term. With depression often manifesting itself in the guise of occasional episodes as opposed to just one long period of sadness and withdrawal, it is therefore necessary for treatment to be continually administered until the signs and symptoms finally disappear. Even after the signs and symptoms are no longer evident, your teen will still need to be constantly monitored to decrease the risk of depression gaining a foothold once again.

Supplemental treatment for depression

As with treating any other sickness, treating depression has a greater likelihood of success if coupled with supplemental measures that reduce the risk of the condition firmly taking root in the patient's system. The good news is these measures won't involve anything that could put your teen's health at risk; neither are they too costly to be implemented regularly.

- *Make sure your teen gets at least 8 hours of uninterrupted sleep every night.* Convince your teen that having a refreshed, well-rested mind and body will give them improved memory and concentration, hence making it harder for depression to maintain its hold on them. If your teen has homework that may require them to pull an all-nighter, firmly but gently remind them that having a healthy mind is more important than getting good grades.

- *Encourage your teen to get at least half an hour of exercise 3 to 5 times a week.* With 10 minutes of physical exercise already proven to release a generous amount of endorphins—the body's "feel good" hormones—into your teen's system, just imagine the world of good that 30 minutes of aerobics, walking the dog, or shooting hoops three times a week can do for them.

- *Make sure your teen eats balanced meals rich in healthy fats and proteins every day to improve brain health.* They should consume more of lean meats, cold water fish, fresh produce, and whole grains and less of sugary foods like candies, chocolate, pasta, and even the so-called "energy" drinks that young people seem to consume by the gallon these days.

- *Get your teen to pick up the habit of meditation or any other mind relaxation technique.* Sitting in a quiet place with no distractions for even just a few minutes each day can help them reorient their focus. They can also use this quiet time to think of all the good things that have happened to them, and concentrate on and be thankful for those instead of entertaining negative thoughts.

Mitigating the risk

In addition to directly treating your teen's depression, you need to ensure a home environment that will also take their condition into account and prevent it from worsening. Even the most effective treatment in the world will be rendered useless if the teen continues to interact in an environment that could do them more harm than good.

The biggest challenge here is that you still need to continually set your teen along the right path for their own benefit. Although you still need to give them the freedom to properly deal with their condition, it shouldn't be excessive to the point that they will engage in just about *anything*, even potentially harmful practices, in the mistaken belief that it can help them keep moving forward on the road to recovery.

The following are steps you need to take to achieve the type of home environment that is conducive for your teen's recovery from depression.

- Give them some breathing room instead of disciplining them right away when they fail to obey instructions properly.

- For now (at least), disciplining your teen should involve positive reinforcement instead of punishment and cruel tone and language that could otherwise cause them to feel even worse.

- Make it clear that, first and foremost, you are there to love them and to listen to them, not to have them listen to you. Otherwise, if you spend every one-on-one meeting with your teen telling them that it's not as bad as they feel, or worse, advising them on what you think is best for them without giving them a chance to speak, you will only make them less willing to open up to you about how they feel.

- Make your teen understand that you are *always* available to listen to them talk about anything that's on their mind.

- Always be the first to initiate conversation with them, especially if they are not yet willing to open up to you. Just don't forget to mention that you are willing to listen more than you are willing to talk.

- Discourage them from using their phone, tablet, or computer as a means of unwinding (This is especially helpful if your teen is a victim of cyberbullying.). Get them started on the habit of reading books and other references with useful information to enrich their minds and to leave less room for negative thoughts to take hold. If they would still rather play games, recommend board games and puzzles that will allow them to practice their creative and analytical thinking.

- If problems at home are among the causes of depression in your teen, you need to do your best to resolve these without aggravating his condition. For example, if your teen is depressed because they often see their parents engaged in a heated argument, then you and your spouse need to find a way to settle your differences without becoming antagonistic—overtly or otherwise—toward each other (Yes, your teen is old enough to identify even the subtle signs of hostility.). If you and your spouse can't come to an agreement just yet, then it would be better for both of you to just avoid contact with each other and stay silent until you have calmed down enough to talk like civilized adults. Remember, your child's well-being will always take precedence over your pride, so learn to be humble enough to make concessions at the right times.

Teenage depression is not impossible to overcome, especially if you regard it as a serious condition and not as just another temporary manifestation of typical juvenile angst. You should therefore learn how to identify the early indicators of it in your teens as well as provide them enough love and encouragement all throughout their treatment and recovery.

Chapter 7. Cyberbullying and How Your Teens Can Overcome It

Due in part to their greater exposure to the online world compared to back when they were younger, teenagers have become highly vulnerable to cyberbullying, which is one of the leading factors contributing to suicides among teens. Thus, it would be unwise for parents to simply ignore it and instruct their children to do the same.

The difference between cyberbullying and "normal" bullying is the fact that in the former, the attacks are virtual rather than corporal in nature. Online posts and comments have taken the place of punches and kicks aimed at where they can deal the most injury. Although the victim's body suffers no bruises, their dignity and self-esteem get hurt just as if they were subjected to physical abuse. You would want your teens to learn how they can think and act for themselves, but when they are faced with something as hurtful as cyberbullying, it may become necessary for you to step in and become directly involved instead of letting them deal with it on their own.

Do not wait for cyberbullying to start affecting your teens. You should instead prevent this problem from escalating until it becomes too late for your teen.

1. *Have your teen explain the situation to you.* If your teens tell you that they are being harassed online (or even if they don't tell you but you have reason to believe that they are being harassed), sit down with them and find out what's going on and why. They may be bullied

because of their physical stature, their race, their religious beliefs, or even utterly trivial reasons like the way they dress. Whatever it is, it should be clear to you so that you will be better able to help your teens overcome the traumatic experience.

2. *Gather as much evidence of it as possible.* One good thing about online interactions is that evidence of it can be easily acquired. Advise your teens to make screen captures of hurtful posts, comments, images, and conversations for future reference.

3. *Guide your teen on how to manage their social media presence.* Instruct your teen to configure the privacy settings on their social media accounts so that only trusted individuals can view and

comment on their posts. Also advise them to avoid common virtual areas such as message boards and public sites, especially those that are frequented by those who keep bullying them. They may even need to stay offline so as to deprive bullies of any opportunities to attack them directly.

4. *Inform the authorities at your teens' school.* Unfortunately, there is little that your teens' school can do against cyberbullying even if the perpetrators are also enrolled there. Teachers and school administrators cannot directly intervene unless incidents of harassment take place on the school premises. Nonetheless, you can still bring the matter to the attention of your teens' teachers and other school officials. At the very least, it could help other

authority figures be aware of what's going on and compel them to keep a close watch on the individuals involved to prevent the situation from getting any worse.

5. *Bring the matter to the attention of local law enforcement.* This is to be done only in extreme cases that may be considered criminal in nature (depending on your state of residence), such as when a bully overtly threatens to inflict actual physical harm or plans to extort the victim for money in exchange for deleting the hurtful posts. Your teen should provide screenshots of these incidents when you ask for help from your local police department, who will then take steps towards bringing the harassment to an end (usually by apprehending the perpetrators and

charging them with the appropriate offenses).

Conclusion

I hope this book was able to enlighten you on the key pointers you need to know to raise your teenaged children so that they will someday become adults who are healthy, confident and able to make wise decisions to take care of themselves.

The next step is to take what you have learned from reading this book and apply it in every day that you spend loving and raising your teens. Remember, a parent is like an artist who takes a blank canvas, uses a variety of colors, and repeatedly makes strokes of different styles and lengths all throughout until they finally come up with a masterpiece that other people will also admire. Hence, if you want your teenagers to be the best possible versions of themselves when they get older, you need to be persistent in providing them the love and the guidance that they need in the here and now.

May you be successful in showing your teenagers the way to becoming mature and responsible adults who can, in their own simple way, make the world a better place for themselves and for others!

Thank you and good luck!